A GOSPEL FOR THE GOLDEN AGE

(Second edition, Revised)

Sathya Sai Baba

and

Jesus Christ

By

Peter Phipps

Illustrations by

Lyn Kriegler

Swami's signature from First
Edition of this book

This book is humbly laid at the Lotus Feet of
Bhagavan Sri Sathya Sai Baba,
whose message and example of Universal Love is
bringing in the Golden Age of God's rule on Earth,
and who has so graciously blessed this book.

The Cross and the Lotus

A symbol for the Golden Age of Unity

Cut 'I' feeling clean across and let your ego
die on the Cross to endow on you Eternity

Be like the lotus, unattached to the slush where in it is born
and the water in which it is bred. Like the lotus,
though you may be in the world, do not
allow the world to get into you and
affect your sense of values
Be in the world but not of it.

PREFACE

For the past many years it has been obvious that love of our fellow man and of all nature has fallen by the wayside and is now grossly overshadowed by mankind's evil tendencies that are rampant throughout the world today. One does not have to search for evidence of this: It can be seen clearly in our everyday life. Wars between countries, civil wars, greed, anger, hatred, jealousy and evil deeds, have become daily occurrences that one is constantly tempted to regard as normal.

Many Christians have asked why God allows all this to happen. The answer, of course, is very simple. Jesus said, *"As ye sow, so shall ye reap"*. God is not the designer of what is happening. It is Man himself who, through his past thoughts, words and deeds, has brought these calamities upon himself

Faced with this state of affairs, many are earnestly praying for the "second coming" so that the world can be changed into a better place in which to live. But it must be understood that it is not the world which has to change. The world is beautiful and provides all things for mankind. It is we who have to change. Only then we will find that there is nothing wrong with the world at all. We may very well be able to quote or recite the Bible or other Scriptures but all this is of no value whatsoever if we do not live the teachings within these Scriptures.

We may ask how we will recognise this "second coming"? If Jesus Himself walked through our neighbourhood today announcing His identity, there would be a great risk of His being stoned or beaten as an imposter. Whatever form our Lord might take, until He becomes recognised and accepted by all, the risk of violent rejection would remain. This book will go a long way towards helping us to open our minds, broaden our vision, and expand our consciousness and understanding.

Two thoughts in particular came to mind when reading the manuscript for the first time. Firstly, that in writing a book of this nature, the author showed himself to be a man of great courage, for, although there will be many within the Christian world who will recognise the Truth, there are sure to be many others who will ridicule or condemn. This sort of adverse reaction will arise because of resistance to the great turn-around of thought that will be necessary for one to accept the content of this book in all its beauty, and to appreciate the enormity of the Truth it reveals so clearly before us.

Secondly, it came through clearly that a man who has as much love for God and all His Creation as Peter's has, could not possibly do otherwise than present these revelations to his fellow man. He has had the courage to do this, so that all may have the opportunity to come to know that God the Father has incarnated and is walking the earth today.

We only have to look at what has been happening in the world over the past many years to know that God would not allow such atrocities, such evil to continue to the point where all mankind could be destroyed. Nor should we limit God by thinking - and even insisting - that He has made only one appearance in human form since this world of ours came into being. Mankind accepts and talks of the Lord appearing on earth some two thousand years ago in the form of our Beloved Jesus, because it has been so written in the Scriptures. But, when He was alive, He was not accepted.

Though it may be difficult to accept that God could appear again in another form, and in our own lifetime, let us not be so complacent, so engrossed in our worldly affairs, that we would hesitate to investigate and find the Truth for ourselves. Let us take this opportunity to ask questions - to investigate these revelations and find out for ourselves.

Wherever we may be be in our present lifetime, we have the opportunity to personally experience the Formless God, that Pure Love which is expressing Itself through the form of Sathya Sai Baba in India today.

His Love is beyond all explanation. In front of such a Love, one immediately becomes aware of the total inadequacy of the spoken word. One cannot be in His Presence and remain unaffected by His Love.

I encourage the reader to read this book in its entirety before expressing an opinion. Dare to be different! Investigate its message in the sure knowledge that there is only one thing which is certain during one's lifetime and that is - change.

Let us not resist the change which is taking place in the world today, but rather put our shoulders to the wheel. The faster the wheel turns, and the more quickly we bring about change within ourselves, the sooner we will have peace in the world and thus live in the Brotherhood of Man and the Fatherhood of God.

Arthur Hillcoat.

ACKNOWLEDGEMENTS

I wish to pay special tribute to a tireless worker for the Lord and good friend, **Madeleine Guillemin** who somehow found the time among all her other work to listen to me, advise me and occasionally prod me in the work on this book, as well as doing the desk-top publishing to get it into its final format. Her friendship and wisdom are greatly appreciated.

I am greatly indebted **to Lyn Kriegler** who has produced the illustrations and had the inspiration for the cover-design for the book, without forgetting **Glen Furguson** who so ably executed that design. Lyn has gone to much effort to obtain all those nice things which would otherwise have left this work as just a lot of text, less attractive to the eyes. I thank her for her interest, enthusiasm and patient effort as well as the way in which she has taken the work to her heart.

A very big thank-you also to **Arthur Hillcoat**, our beloved 'White Lion', who has touched me deeply with the beautiful preface that he has written.

Last but not least, I wish to thank all my **friends and colleague**s who have encouraged me in preparing this book, for helpful comments and suggestions. Not all agreed with the contents, and I welcomed this, as it is often in disagreements that the important issues can be explored. Many of their ideas have been adopted, so the authorship of this book is widespread, but the responsibility for any errors or faults must lie with myself.

Mata Betty took a draft of this work to Prasanthi Nilayam to present to Sathya Sai Baba in August 1993, and her encouraging news that "Swami" had blessed the draft led to the decision to publish the book. I acknowledge the quiet support of this most gracious devotee. Thanks are due to the following people for permission to use copyright material:

To **Sri Sathya Sai Books and Publications Trust**, Prasanthi Nilayam, for the many quotes from Sathya Sai Baba.

To Gateway Books, for permission to use a chapter from *"Sathya Sai Baba Embodiment of Love"* By Peggy Mason and Ron Laing and, above all, to **Ron Laing** himself who so kindly signed that permission himself shortly before leaving this life.

To dear **Jack Hislop** for giving me a similar permission to use a chapter from his book *"My Baba and I"* and to Birth Day Publishing Co for their endorsement of same.

To **Howard Murphet** for permission to use a chapter from his book, "Sai Baba Avatar" and **Rev Robert Pipes** for the use of his article originally published in "Golden Age 1980" by Sri Sathya Sai Books and Publications Trust, who also gave their permission for its use.

Above all, I must express my love and gratitude to **Bhagavan Sathya Sai Baba**, for allowing me to be His instrument in putting this book together. This book is laid at His Lotus Feet in humble appreciation for all the blessings He bestows on all Creation so freely. Without His inspiration, guidance and blessing, this book would never have been written. Not only has He been my inspiration throughout, but in February 1994 when I had the great good fortune of an interview, He further blessed it by signing the front page of the proof-copy. THANK YOU. That *"With love Baba"* in His own hand, has meant more to me than anything else in the world.

OM SAI RAM!

TABLE OF CONTENTS

LIST OF PHOTOGRAPHS

INTRODUCTION

"Jesus, who attempted to rebuild mankind on the basis of Love, was crucified by little men who feared that their tiny towers of hate and greed would be toppled by His teaching. . . . No one who has trodden this path and engaged himself in (this) process has escaped calumny and cruelty. Those who seek to know God must steel themselves to bear insult and injury with a smile"

Sathya Sai Baba

We live in a time when Christians are expecting the imminent return of Christ; when other religions are expecting the return or incarnation of their form of Deity, and many other people, often with no religious or spiritual beliefs at all, are talking of a "New Age", a time when the world changes fundamentally and a new world order is established. There are occult traditions around the supposed significance of this New Age featured in many bookstores and popular magazines.

Some people look to the "New Age" as a time when there will be a new political order which will favour their group over another, or as a time when everyone can do as they like, free from the restrictions of old traditions which are being thrown away. Other people, including many Christians, consider the "New Age" is a term for the destruction of morality and the overthrow of Christianity and other traditional values by forces of darkness. The term "New Age" in such circles has negative associations.

This book accepts that there will be a New Age, and that its coming is as inevitable as the day which follows the night. However, for various reasons, the term "Golden Age" is preferred over "New Age". The reasons include firstly, the fact that the term "New Age" has strong negative associations to many people; secondly that when the significance of what God is presently doing among us is fully understood we will see that it is truly Golden; and thirdly that this is the actual term used by the Great Teacher of the Age, Sri Sathya Sai Baba, Christ Incarnate, the inspiration for this work.

I am writing in the certain knowledge that the Christian Church (including all the separate churches) is about to face the biggest challenge and most sweeping changes in its history. While the Church may feel secure with its tradition reaching back nearly 2,000 years to Jesus Christ and the apostles, and its roots in the scriptures as compiled in the fourth and fifth centuries A.D., it will inevitably be overtaken by the "Golden Age" and changed almost beyond recognition. This process will be well under way within 30 years and has indeed already quietly started.

I happen to be one of many thousands of fortunate Christians around the world who have had a vision of the approaching Golden Age and can see the shape of the future in general terms. The evidence is clear for those "with ears to hear and eyes to see". I hope in this book either to present sufficient evidence to justify the claims which are made, or point the reader to where the evidence may be found.

I feel myself to be in the position of one looking out to sea and watching a tidal wave gathering momentum and size as it nears the shore. I invite others to look in the direction in which I am looking, and prepare themselves for its arrival. We are helpless to prevent its arrival, just as King Canute could not turn back a much lesser tide. When those who have not seen its approach are suddenly overwhelmed by it, there will be much surprise and shock. Those who are prepared for it will suffer much less. The tidal wave will strike Christendom within ten years, perhaps much sooner. After it strikes, Christianity will be renewed and transformed, and Christians will truly be among those who are the salt of the Earth and light to the world.

No doubt there will be great resistance to the changes, and much anguish. The pain and conflict can be lessened when the Nature of the changes are understood. That is why I have written this book. In this book it is argued that the Golden Age commences with the return of Christ to His Kingdom on Earth. Another way of looking at it is that the work which Jesus began will find its fruition when the Gospel will truly be preached to all the nations. These times are predicted in the Bible, and in many other Scriptures on the Earth.

The Second Coming of Christ (as Christians would call it) will result in true reforms within the church, a restoration of the full message of Jesus, without the errors which have crept in to Christian doctrine, and the flowering of God's Kingdom on Earth. The process is starting already in quiet ways, and is gathering momentum gently but steadily. By the time those who would resist the changes become aware of them, the momentum will be unstoppable. Jesus warned us that the coming of the Lord will be as a "thief in the night". If He is with us now and we ignore His presence, we will wake up in the morning to find the house has been turned over and we did not hear a thing. Worse still, if we are too late in our awakening, He will have already left the house and we will have missed the chance to meet Him.

Unlike other thieves, this is One whose presence we should welcome. Those people alive today have an opportunity which is unique in history, as we have the chance to see the Lord, and perhaps even meet Him face-to-face and talk with Him. Future generations of our descendants will envy the opportunity we have now, though we may not realize it.

For those who greet such claims with skepticism and disbelief, all I can hope to do is to present the evidence for these claims and show Christians why they should welcome the advent of the Golden Age.

The Coming of the Christ

When someone claims to be the Christ what are we to make of the claim? We have been warned by Jesus in Matthew 24: 4, 5

> *"Beware that no one leads you astray. For many will come in my name, saying, 'I am the Messiah!' and they will lead many astray."*[1]

There have already been many false prophets, false messiahs and false claimants to be the Second Christ. Clearly it would be a mistake to chase after every plausible rogue who claims to be Christ. How will we know the difference between all these charlatans and the genuine Christ? It may seem the safe thing to do to cast doubt on all claimants, and to assume that anyone who claims to be the Christ is a fraud. However, this course, too, carries a significant risk. It is a great cost to us if we follow after a false Christ. However, it would be equally as big a loss for us if we fail to recognise the Christ when He does come. Could it be that our great-grandchildren will say:

> *"What an opportunity they missed! Christ walked on Earth in their time and they knew Him not".*

These questions have to be asked, and with some urgency. We need to know how to tell the difference between a false Christ and the real one, for we may soon have to make such a decision. If we know how we are going to make it, then it will be so much less painful for us.

The Test of the Anti-Christ

Supposing you were to hear of someone whom people tell you is the Christ. How would you know whether the person giving you the news

---

[1] * All quotations from the Bible, unless specified otherwise, are from the New Revised Standard Version

was deluded, misguided, or correct? What would you expect Christ to look like? What would He or She do?

Let us suppose that Christ is already walking the Earth, and you were to meet Him or Her. How would you know who this person is? If you knew He raised the dead, healed the sick, and performed other miracles as Jesus did, including feeding crowds by multiplying food, turning water into petrol, walking on water and so on, would you believe this person is the Christ?

Such a person clearly has supernatural powers, but would you suspect sorcery, demonic powers, or even that this person is one of the anti-christs, which may be first suspicion? Let us look at the anti-christ theory. This is what John says about the last days and the anti-christ:

> *"Children, it is the last hour. As you have heard that antichrist is coming, so now many antichrists have come. From this we know that it is the last hour. . . . Who is the liar but the one who denies that Jesus is the Christ? <u>This is the antichrist, the one who denies the Father and the Son;</u> everyone who confesses the Son has the Father also."* (I John 2 : 18-23, abridged)

So here we have one clear test for the anti-christ; someone who denies the Father and the Son. Clearly we must expect that the Second Christ will not deny the Father or the Son, but will affirm both.

A second clear test is given by Jesus:

> *"Beware of false prophets who come to you in sheep's clothing but inwardly are ravening wolves. <u>You will know them by their fruits.</u>"* (Matthew 7 : 15,16)

The fruits of Sathya Sai Baba are that He has set the very highest standards of virtue in education, medicine, government and other fields of human conduct; He has inspired many thousands of people to live a God-fearing and saintly life; and His teachings represent the highest level of ethics and spirituality. Evil men do not inspire others to be saints. His own life and conduct is fully consonant with His own teachings. No person can point to any evil deed done by Sathya Sai Baba, while there are literally millions of testimonies to good deeds that He has done.

The Coming of God Prophesied in Other Faiths

What else would we expect of the Second Christ? Would He or She affirm Christianity only, or would the Christ look into the hearts of all people regardless of creed, race, social position and gender? Would this person be accepted by Buddhists, Hindus, Moslems and others, or are Christians the only ones expecting Him?

Let us look at prophecies from other faiths:

From the American Red Indians, Black Elk lived before the coming of the white man, whose coming he foresaw. He also told of the coming of a new age, and a messenger of love and understanding who would bring the entire human race into a circle of love and harmony. Black Elk said that when people received this new message, those who understood it would be like flames of fire spreading it to other people, but those who did not receive the new message would be filled with darkness.

The one we know as the Buddha said:

> *"I am not the first Buddha who has come upon the Earth, nor shall I be the last. In due time another Buddha will arise in the world; a Holy One, a supremely enlightened One, endowed with wisdom, embracing the Universe, an incomparable leader of men, a ruler of angels and mortals, he will reveal to you the same eternal truths which I have taught to you"*

It is told in Buddhist prophecies how the new Era shall manifest itself starting with an unprecedented war among nations, with brother against brother and lack of understanding between peoples. In this respect, Buddha says much the same things which Jesus tells us.

Hindus have a tradition of Divine incarnations who come to restore harmony, peace and righteousness among peoples. One of their Scriptures, the Mahabharata, tells of a Kaliyuga, corresponding to our present age, marked by moral and spiritual decline, political corruption, oppression, dishonesty, crime and the prevalence of falsehood. Vishnu said:

> *"When evil is rampant upon the earth, I will take birth in the family of a virtuous man and assume a human body to restore tranquillity. This avatar will possess great energy, great intelligence and great powers. He will restore order and peace in the world, he will inaugurate a new era of truth and will be adored by spiritual people."*

Mohammed tells of "the Guided One" who is to come, who will have great power, great wisdom and knowledge. Mohammed gives a list of 300 features including a very clear physical description of the "Guided One". Mohammed says, among many other things he who will be short, live for 96 years, be highly intelligent, be surrounded by many followers, have profuse hair, wear red robes, have a mole on the cheek, and so on.

Mohammed also says that Moslems will not recognise Him until 9 years before His passing from the Earth and adds "You could have stretched out your hand and touched Him, but you missed Him".

In the West, Nostradamus predicted that after the Battle of Armageddon a new saviour will appear to guide people in the way of Truth and Peace. In the Book of Revelation there are similar prophecies.

Jews, of course, are still awaiting their Messiah.

The interesting point from all this is that the coming of a person Christians would call the Christ is expected by most people of the world. It therefore is to be expected that such a person will be eventually accepted by all spiritual peoples of whatever religion or creed.

This, then, is the second test I would make of a claimant to be the Christ. Not only must He or She affirm Jesus as Christ, but also will be accepted by other religions which have teachings compatible with those of Christ. From our traditional perspective it may seem a tall order, but it will be seen that Sathya Sai Baba passes both tests.

The Need for the Current Incarnation of Christ

We need to realize that God does not come to Earth unless He has to. Jesus said:

> *"And you will hear of wars and rumors of wars; see that you are not alarmed; for this must take place, but the end is not yet. For nation will rise up against nation, and kingdom against kingdom, and there will be famines and earthquakes in various places: all this is but the beginning of birth-pangs."* (Matthew 24 : 5-8)

There is much talk among Christians of the Battle of Armageddon which is mentioned in the Book of Revelation (16:16), and reads very much like a nuclear war. I believe that the Battle of Armageddon in the form of nuclear war between nations will not happen on Earth, and it is to prevent such a war that Christ has come in the form of Sathya Sai Baba. There is in fact evidence that the Lord has already intervened to prevent such a war.

It is also arguable that the Battle of Armageddon is even now occurring in the spiritual realms beyond our mortal sight, which is why we seem to have so many people, including our political leaders and others who are doing work which could be demonic in origin. Crime and immorality is now rampant, and the Governments of the world seem powerless to stop it, and even encourages it, as the idea that economic values are paramount over human values is widely adopted.

In New Zealand, as many other countries who have adopted "the market economy" as their route to salvation, we are saddled with a political and economic system which is destroying moral values, setting class against class and encouraging the most pernicious of enterprises in the form of casinos. The willingness of neighbour to help neighbour is being destroyed and there is a noticeable hardening of hearts against the needy and hungry. The greedy and unscrupulous are rewarded and those who raise moral objections are scorned as unrealistic or preaching a discredited Gospel. In a land of plenty, there are children who are not being fed, families who cannot afford medical care and thousands of young people who can see no solution to their problems except for suicide. Surely the forces of darkness are succeeding in temporarily taking over what used to be called Paradise. We are experiencing the consequences of unbridled ego and selfishness in all aspects of our life.

The only alternative to this slide into Hell on Earth is an acceptance of the ways of Righteousness, Truth, Love, Inner Peace and Non-Violence. It is these values which Sathya Sai Baba brings to us. The forces of darkness will succeed only temporarily. This was prophesied in the Bible and is reinforced by Sathya Sai Baba.

The free-market economy is not itself causing the economic difficulties being felt in most countries of the world. The free market philosophy has freed humanity from the deadening stranglehold of Government and political ideologies and may be a potent force for good, when managed from a spiritual perspective. The destructive forces arise when the free market is used only for the enrichment of the few at the expense of the rest. When spiritual values motivate the free market, which they will do in the future, then the world will enjoy a period of prosperity and peace which has never before been seen in the history of the human race.

Yet another possibility is that the Battle of Armageddon is actually occurring within the human soul at this time when so many people live hopeless lives of misery, degradation and Godlessness. Just because many people are living in hard times, they do not have to live in misery. Even the rich are often miserable. Poverty and misery are often states of mind, rather than objective experience.

However bleak the world seems to be at present, be assured that good will triumph over evil. What we see now are, as Jesus tells us, "birth-pangs".

Acceptance of the Second Christ by the Churches

It is only a matter of time before the churches will have to accept that the Lord has come again. It may be a gradual evolutionary awakening in that as more Christians accept Sathya Sai Baba as Lord and serve to leaven the churches from within, the message spreads by word of mouth slowly, or it may come suddenly when a "critical mass" (to use an analogy from nuclear physics) of Christians are receptive to the Lord and a sudden change in Christian consciousness will take place overnight. My reading of prophecy and the guidance of my own meditations tells me that the latter option is the more likely, though the leavening process is already occurring. There are now significant numbers of Christians, including some clergy, active in their own churches, who accept Sathya Sai Baba as Lord at one with Jesus Christ. In my considered opinion, by the end of this decade, I expect the churches, beginning perhaps with the Church of Rome in concert with the Orthodox tradition, to announce that they acknowledge that Christ is with us now.

When meditating upon this matter as to when the change will happen, I had a vision of the Berlin Wall collapsing, as it did, literally overnight. The Berlin Wall was taken down when a whole people had a shift of consciousness and collectively decided that this monument to political insanity had to go. The leaders of the people had also lost the will to oppose the popular action. My vision suggested that a similar shift will soon occur within Christendom.

The Reaction of Christians

When the Advent of the Lord is formally recognized by church leaders I expect a great upheaval in the churches. Most Christians will react with shock, disbelief and denial. There will be a lot of pain and perhaps a sense of betrayal. Inevitably many will refuse to accept the news and will wonder whether the Anti-Christ has taken over the Church. Despite what our ecclesiastical leaders tell us, we will each have to make up our own minds. Could our leaders be misled? How will we know?

If we ourselves have a clear idea as to how to discriminate between a false Christ and the real one, we will save ourselves much needless pain, and give ourselves the opportunity to see Him on Earth.

Sathya Sai Baba

In this book it is claimed that the Lord has already returned and is with us on Earth now in the form of Sathya Sai Baba, presently living on the outskirts of a little village in South India called Puttaparthi. This book is addressed specifically for Christians to provide information to make up their own minds. While I can produce great amounts of evidence to support the claims made, these do not constitute proof until you, the reader, accept the evidence as true. Ultimately it remains for your own heart to tell you whether you find the evidence convincing.

Different people are convinced of the Divinity of Sathya Sai Baba in different ways. Some meet Him in dreams or meditation. Some meet Him through healing of physical or mental disorders. I met Him when counseling survivors of the Aramoana massacre. I was confirmed in my faith in Him when I looked into His eyes. The following meditation is based upon my experience sitting on the ground in front of the mandir at Puttaparthi:

A VISION OF GOD

He walked by me every day, the one they call the Christ.

He blessed some, ignored others, I don't know why.

I wanted to meet His eyes, to see the face of God.

But He did not see me,

He saw everyone else, not me, why not me?

Then one day, one wonderful day, He stood close by.

I gazed into His face and for a moment,
His eyes met mine.

In those eyes was infinity,
More profound than space,
More potent than the Sun,
All knowing, all seeing.

Like Adam I was naked before Him.
He saw me, what I am, what I could be,
What I have attained, and where I have failed.
He saw my past, my present and my future.
He saw all my sins and blemishes.
My ego and my pride.

He saw also what I can be in Him,
If only I surrender to Him,
To give up my faults and errors,
My ego and my pride.
His eyes held compassion for sorrows I bring on myself.
His eyes held Love for me despite who I am.
His eyes held the Universe and all of us in it.

In His eyes I recognized my God,
My Creator, my Master.
I saw also myself reflected as the image of God.

I felt my soul being drawn into His eyes,
As if in a moment I could be one with Him,
Not the petty self any more,
But a new creature in whom God shines forth.

Then His eyes looked away,
And my life was changed.
For one eternal, precious moment I saw Divinity.
I saw God, and He saw me.
His eyes turned away, but He still sees me.

CHAPTER ONE

MY PERSONAL TESTIMONY

"Call Me by any name ---- Krishna, Allah, Christ. Can't you recognize me in any form? Continue your worship of your chosen God along the lines familiar to you and you'll find you are coming near to Me, for all Names and Forms are Mine"

Sathya Sai Baba

When devotees of Sathya Sai Baba meet, a common question asked *is "How did you come to know of Sai Baba?"* More often than not, the answer to the question is through a miracle. This was certainly so in my case, and so here is my story.

My origins are within a fairly traditional Christian setting, having being raised as an Anglican, confirmed by Geoffrey Fisher, then Archbishop of Canterbury, and having struggled with my faith for years. At one stage I had applied for admission to Holy Orders (Anglican terminology for ordination as a priest), and came within six weeks of admission to theological college before a letter from my vicar to the bishop led to an abandonment of these plans. However, I maintained my interest, and continued to study theology and comparative religions.

My faith waxed and waned over the years. I felt compelled to believe in God as a logical probability, but had little sense of a personal relationship with the Deity. I believed in a Creator, but not the personal guide, friend and Heavenly Father whom I have now come to know.

I qualified as a psychologist in the early 1960's and worked within the prison system, marketing research industry, the New Zealand Army and private practice before I joined The Salvation Army as a salaried employee. I still believed in a Creator, but could find little evidence that He (or She) took a personal interest in what we do any more than the force of gravity distinguishes between people.

Then my life and belief system changed, literally between one day and the next. The following account was written shortly after the events described:

> *On 13 November 1990 at Aramoana, near Dunedin, David Gray had an argument with his neighbor, Gary Holden. Gray then took a rifle, shot Gary Holden and then killed 12 more people before being gunned down by the Police nearly 24 hours later. Altogether 14 people died, including Police Sergeant Stuart Guthrie.*

> *I was one of a team of three on a Crisis Intervention Team sent into the area on 14 November to counsel victims. The others were Betty Rasmussen and Babs Miller (as leader). We were part of a Victim's Task Force established for that purpose. We arrived at Dunedin Hospital as the bodies were brought in for identification by the families and the body count still unknown. The air was full of grief and confusion.*

> *Thus begins the most harrowing and yet spiritual two and a half days of my life. We counseled over 100 people between us,*

as victims told us their story and received affirmation for their feelings. They then became survivors. We saw victory over tragedy again and again.

We had all attended a course at the Royal Police College some two weeks earlier on how to cope with just this type of event. The course leaders, Marlene Young and Karen McLaughlin had been to Dunedin the week before the incident and briefed Police and Salvation Army workers on coping with crises. Some say the timing was "providential", it was certainly for-tunate as it provided the knowledge necessary for handling New Zealand's biggest mass murder.

We have accepted such violence in Beirut or Northern Ireland and have become immunised to it. I now know that such horror affects real people who also weep. The world does not have to be so unloving and hateful. The team learned that with love all things seem possible. I had the sense that this Earth could be Paradise if only we loved one another. The gospel seems so practical, so "here and now", so non-mystical. Heaven does not have to be in another plane or another place, we already have it, if we only knew it.

All of us on the team felt that we were operating with a power beyond our own. The energy available to us was phenomenal! We knew that others were praying for us and thinking about us, and this helped, particularly when we got a message of support from Marlene and Karen. The power seemed mightier than that available at most times.

I felt that the power of Christ was available to us directly, and it contained wisdom, power, love and caring. We manifested all those things to others, yet "not I, but Christ who worketh through me". Had we let our egos get in the way, the power would not have flowed as it did. The job was too important to get personally involved with ego.

On the second morning I woke up with the thought that the easy way of working using (or being used by) a higher power was the way that Jesus must have worked. The whole Christian story made sense at a higher level than before, and I felt that most Christians do not understand Christianity. Formalised Christianity destroys the essence of what Jesus was saying. When Jesus brings life more abundantly it is for our sakes, not his, and he does not need our thanks as the act is sufficient in itself.

We saw people turn around from a state of confusion and shock to positive action. It is difficult to write of what we did without it seeming self-serving or grandiose. It was a very healing power for which we were but channels. What we learned is that there is a vast reserve of power available when it is needed. It is not our power, but we may use it. It seemed to flow through us when we dealt with people, it healed and comforted.

At the time we all shed (and shared) copious tears and relied upon each other for support. Every time we thought of the suffering and misery we wept. I have shed most of my tears for now, but when I tell my story people still weep to hear it. Some people have told us we were wonderful, but we do not feel at all wonderful, rather that we have access to a wonderful power which we may rightly call the Holy Spirit.

What we feel is the great privilege to have been of use to others and to the Lord. In this form of service we gained so much in spiritual insight and experience that the help given to others through us seems small enough. And yet we know that but for the intervention given through us the hurt would have been much greater than it was.

At one level all we did was ask people to tell us their story and check through their feelings, safety and ongoing personal support. We arranged practical support when required such as housing and having people overseas informed of the safety of victims.

At a different level we seemed to be directly touching the spirit of people and providing the knowledge they needed to heal themselves.

Our final act was to go out to Aramoana and hold a little service on the site of the Holden's house fire and to pray for the victims. We were all broken up with grief, but it seemed a good way to end our part in the tragedy. Within a very few feet of us so many people had died and the ground was still literally drenched with their blood.

On the way home after the events described above, I thanked God in my heart for the help He provided, and I got a very clear reply:

"I am greater than you know, seek me out and find me."

This message implied that there was the possibility of finding the source of the message, and so I determined to explore and find the Source. I had had the sense for a long time that Jesus was not fully revealed in the teachings of the churches or in the Gospels of the New Testament. Somehow the essence of the Man we call Jesus and the Revelation of the God seemed a bit misty.

In a later account of my journey to Sai Baba, I wrote the following account for a friend:

I was intrigued at what is called "the missing years of Jesus". Some church people assume He was an ordinary carpenter, following in His earthly father's footsteps. I wanted to find the truth. Jesus at Aramoana was so strong a presence I could feel His heart beating with mine. I sensed a Being of infinite Love, strength, and beauty of character. I wanted to know this Man, and so I wanted to seek Him out. I understood from the message that He is available to be found.

In search of the deeper truths I started in a bookshop dealing in esoteric texts. My intention was to sift through everything I could find, no matter what the origin, and use my discrimination to sort out the truth from the bizarre. I had had such a taste of Jesus that I was confident of knowing the difference. In the bookshop, one text nearly leaped into my hand. I saw it on the shelf, a book called "The Jesus Mystery", by Richard and Janet Bock. My hand grew very warm when I reached for it, and I was confident it would help me.

The book gives an account of Christ's missing years, drawing heavily on a work discovered in a Tibetan monastery by Nicolas Notovitch in 1887. It also quotes supporting material from India which would appear to confirm the account given in Notovitch's manuscript which traces the journeys of Jesus to Persia, India and Tibet. It tells of Jesus having to flee for His life after the Jains objected to Him giving spiritual instruction to Sudras (Untouchables). Similarly, Jesus also offended the Buddhists at a later time.

The book then stated that Jesus is written as "Issa" in Tibet and "Isa" in Indian languages, and means "Divine Mother". The same term can also be written as "Sai". The book then suggested that Sathya Sai Baba, a modern spiritual teacher in India, is the prophesied returned Lord come to save mankind from the present crisis. "Sathya" means "Truth"; the name "Baba" is said to be the same as "Abba", which Jesus used when addressing the Father.

Being interested in such a claim, I followed it through, reading very critically a number of books on Sai Baba, hoping to find some fault which would disprove the thesis. I actually wanted to prove it false, as the implications for it being true are so overwhelming. Instead, I was impressed with the consistency of accounts given of this man. When so many people affirm the same story, whether Indian, American, English, Australian or New Zealanders, Christian, Hindu, Buddhist or Jewish, there is reason to accept that they all bear witness to the same things.

It was claimed that Sathya Sai Baba has raised the dead on several occasions; heals all manner of diseases daily; sometimes feeds crowds by multiplying available food; demonstrates knowledge of the past, present and future of everyone; and is often experienced as pure Love. He is said to speak all languages in the world, without having studied them; knows all Scriptures but does not read books; has turned water into petrol several times, and even whisky into water when one person tried to smuggle the latter into His ashram.

I prayed about all this and received some wonderful answers to prayer. I also found in my work with clients some rather miraculous things were happening. In my work I tend to have the more difficult clients, and on several occasions when all the techniques I knew had failed I turned to silent prayer and found an answer. I asked the Lord how should I know when to work psychologically, and when spiritually. The answer was clear: "Stop working psychologically and work only spiritually".

After a while I noticed a pattern in the help the Lord was giving me. All problems which humans find in their lives arise in the first place from faulty ideas, including attachment to things, the sense of ego and selfishness. The pattern which I was given involves finding the idea which is behind the problem and neutralising it. Traditional counselling generally involves strengthening the ego to add new skills so the counsellee may cope better with his or her problems. The approach I was being led into involves subtracting from the ego so that the client no longer has so strong an impediment to spirituality. At Aramoana I learned that the ego is what separates us from God. By systematically weakening the power of the ego and false ideas, the person becomes free to find God in his life. The logic is wonderfully simple, though people trained in Western psychology would be appalled at such a statement. This is because psychology confuses the reality, which is our God-given nature, with unreality, which is what we have added to our nature. The ego is part of the unreality. When the confusion is resolved the path to liberation is opened.

While all this was going on, my own belief system was undergoing a thorough shake-up, and at times I had to doubt my own sanity. What was happening was contrary to all I had been taught and what everyone else around me "knew". The step from believing in the possibility of God to experiencing the power of His presence is profound enough. When He asks you to give up the familiar way of working to work in totally new ways which you have never heard of before, you have to be very sure of the guidance. You have to know how to discriminate between the imaginings of the mind and the in-tuition from the Lord. I found that whenever I did as I was led, the results were always positive.

It seemed important for me to meet this Sathya Sai Baba if possible and so I joined a trip to India to spend some time at His ashram. If He really is the Lord returned to earth, I wanted to check first-hand for myself.

Just before leaving for India I was giving a lecture to Salvation Army Officer Cadets on basic psychology. It was a talk I have given several times before with no problem. I was in the middle of my introduction when I realized I no longer believed in what I was saying. It was also clear that the cadets did not believe what I was saying either. It was an awful feeling! What happened next was literally inspiration. I turned the diagram of Maslow's Hierarchy of Needs on its head and spoke of spirituality as the basis of Man's existence, not the "nice to have" end when all other needs are satisfied.

It was new material to me. At the time it seemed so radical, I was reluctant to use it, but had no choice. The cadets loved it and related it readily to the teachings of Jesus, but I was somewhat shaken by it. It is scary when you have no idea what you are going to say next.

My experience in India was right out of Biblical times. To see subsistence farming as Jesus would have seen it, herds of goats foraging for food on poor soil, primitive irrigation techniques as used thousands of years ago, and real desert communities was somehow exciting in its novelty.

In the remoteness of a desert area is a village called Puttaparthi, with 800 local people. Associated with the village is a university, secondary and primary school system, where pupils come from all over India to be trained in spiritual values and then sent out as potential future leaders of the nation. I saw an international airport nearing completion, as soon it is expected that crowds of people will fly directly into Puttaparthi on pilgrimage. There is a modern hospital with technology rivalling the best which the USA can produce and designed to set the standard for medicine in India for the next 1000 years. I saw a thoroughly modern planetarium where the story of creation is told and shown; a sophisticated Museum of World Religion; the "Poornachandra", which is one of the wonders of modern architecture in being able to seat 30,000 people without a pillar inside.

I was privileged to see over the University. It is staffed by some of the leading academics of India and the world. They work without pay seven days a week without stress. The University has a spectrometer for measuring the chemical structure of organic compounds is involved in some amazing research which combines both scientific and spiritual principles. I saw the most extraordinary design for a library which maximizes natural light for the readers and minimizes light which fall on the books on the shelves. The computer section was a work of art, being designed according to highly advanced ergonomic principles to minimize strain on operators.

Every part of the design of these facilities is supervised by Sathya Sai Baba, who shows incredible intelligence in these matters.

Assembled for Christmas celebrations were 20,000 people from all countries in the world and most of the world's faiths. The trip was essentially a spiritual pilgrimage, and we learned a lot about Sai Baba's teachings through study of His books, lectures for foreign visitors, discussions with others and hearing His discourses.

We heard a lot about the Golden Age of Sai, which will be a thousand years of peace, justice, righteousness and love. While the talk of "Golden Age" or "New Age" is threatening to some Christians, it should not be, as it is to do with the long-awaited Second Coming. Many Christian errors will be corrected, but the Christian faith will have a new vitality restored to it as its essential truths are affirmed.

At the ashram one heard constantly about miracles performed, people healed and extraordinary phenomena. I saw Sai Baba manifesting vibhuthi (sacred ash with healing and spiritual properties) with a wave of His hand several times. At His orphanage at Srirangapatna I saw vibhuthi forming on pictures of Sai Baba, as I also saw in Singapore. This phenomenon occurs all over the world, including New Zealand. Several of our group closely witnessed Sai Baba manifest a japamala (rosary beads) with a wave of His hand and others saw signet rings being manifested. There is no trickery in these feats, as they are seen to form in the air under His hand.

The discipline was fairly strict, but not harsh. No smoking or alcohol in the ashram; no idle talk; no mixing between the sexes; separate eating, queuing and seating for each sex. All this has a spiritual purpose.

I came away convinced that Sathya Sai Baba is the Lord as prophesied in Chapter 19 of the Book of Revelation. I saw a man whose name is Truth (Sathya means "truth" in His language, Telugu); crowned with many crowns (his hair is unlike any other Indian, each hair being described as a crown in its own right); whose eyes could sometimes be a flame of fire (when I looked into His eyes, I saw an infinity vaster than space); He wears red robes, sometimes the colour of blood; rides in cars (horses?) which are often white; out of whose mouth proceeds a two-edged sword (His words really do smite all nations just read His discourses); He is often surrounded by "armies dressed in fine white linen" (the preferred dress at Puttaparthi, which I was privileged to wear). He has a name which once only He knew, and the story of His announcement of His name is itself marvelous.

Sai Baba says that he has not come to create a new religion, but to revive the old ones, "to make a Christian a better Christian, a Moslem a better Moslem, and a Hindu a better Hindu". He will not disturb anyone in their faith, but confirm them in what they have. He says all names of God are His, all prayers come to Him, and all faiths are His. He compares Himself to a gold merchant, when He judges us he looks only for the amount of gold in our hearts and cares not whether the gold is in the shape of a cross, a Buddha or any God. He returns again and again to the theme that developing love for God and our neighbours is our fundamental task as humans. He constantly states that the heart is mightier than the head, spirituality is higher than theology. He uses many of the terms and phrases Jesus did.

Many Christians have gone to Puttaparthi to prove Sai Baba is the Antichrist, and come away with the opposite opinion. How could the Antichrist validate and enliven the teachings of Jesus and show such infinite Love?

You may wonder why it is that such incredible news is not heard everywhere today, why are there not millions of people going to Puttaparthi instead of a few thousand?

The fact is that Sai Baba does not seek publicity as it would interfere with His main mission. He does not want to attract sensation-seekers or to create resistance. However, I believe the time is near when the whole Earth will hear of Him and His work, although it may take several centuries before the world fully realizes His significance.

I have found Christ to be indeed greater than I know. I am closely involved with my own church and am a lay minister, regularly conducting Church services. I believe I have a greater understanding of Christ than most Christians and have actually been in His physical presence. The mission which I feel I am being called to undertake is to help Christians prepare for the acceptance of the Second Coming. I preach Christ in the form in which Christians know Him, but from the perspective of His teachings in the Golden Age.

The basic message is eternal. It was taught by Christ and Buddha as well as Krishna, Rama and others. The message is essentially as Jesus gave us in the Sermon on the Mount and stresses the Unity of all Creation, the Fatherhood of God and the Brotherhood of Man. His teachings are magnificent in their scope and form, as well as appropriateness for this age. He encourages science when undertaken from a spiritual perspective and in His universities encourages research which will deepen the understanding of Mankind into the real nature of Creation. Sathya Sai Baba has affirmed the truth about Jesus of the manuscript discovered by Notovitch.

Since writing the above letter, I have been to Prashanti Nilayam again and have found new riches and blessings in Sathya Sai Baba, the Christ for the Golden Age. Every day is a new beginning with the Lord as your Companion.

NOTES:

(1) *"The Jesus Mystery"* by Richard and Janet Beck; Aura Books, a division of Aura Enterprises. First published 1980

(2) See Book of Revelation, ch 19: v. 14

Life is a pilgrimage to God; the holy spot is there, afar! The road lies before you; but unless you take the first step forward and follow that step with others, how can you reach it? Start with courage, faith, joy and steadiness. You are bound to succeed. The mind and the intellect are two bullocks tied to a cart, "the inner man". The bullocks are not used to the road of Sathya, Dharma, Santhi and Prema and so they drag the cart along the road familiar to them, namely, Falsehood, Injustice, Worry and Hatred. You have to train them to take the better road so that they may not bring disaster to themselves, the cart they are yoked to and the men inside it.

Sathya Sai Baba

CHAPTER TWO

WHAT IS THE "GOLDEN AGE"?

"Wisdom flashes like lightning amidst the clouds of the inner sky; one has to foster the flash and preserve the light. That is the true sign of the 'educated' person. Do not believe that mastery of many tonnes of books make you wise. Wisdom can grow only where humility prevails. It thrives when man is afraid of vice and sin, and is attached to the Divine in himself, and in all else."

Sathya Sat Baba

Before clarifying the significance of the "Golden Age" it is worthwhile to examine firstly the meaning of the term "New Age".

"New Age" means many things to different people. To some it is a liberation from the shackles of the past, and a chance to discover one's real self (however that is understood). To others it implies a meaningless wallow in ill-formed and fuzzy ideas.

Prophets of the New Age have had an inkling of some massive changes about to occur in relationships and human consciousness. My own understanding of the term "New Age" comes from astrologers, with whom Christians have had a closer association in history than they often care to admit. Astrologers have identified the Christian period with the constellation of Pisces ("the fish"), and the fish was taken as the symbol for Christ by early Christians. About this time in our history (there seems to be no agreement as to exactly when this is happening, although the year 2010 seems to be favoured by many writers) astrologers say that we are moving from Pisces into the constellation of Aquarius, and hence the New Age is described as "Aquarian" or "the Age of Aquarius".

The expectations of the "New Agers" of the 1960's were expressed in the words of a musical called "Hair", which featured a song called "Aquarius", which suggested that the Aquarian Age is a time when there will be "true liberation" of the human mind. The words of the song expressed a truth, but the truth was generally misunderstood. Another song in the play was in praise of sexual deviance, and the play itself made its greatest dramatic impact through the free use of socially proscribed four-lettered words.

The Aquarian Age is expected by the astrologers to be one of enlightenment, peace and spirituality. Some speak of a new "Golden Age", when people will follow a path of righteousness, truth, peace and love. Such Golden Ages are reputed to have happened in the past, but modern people feel less affinity for what they may call mere "pipe dreams".

Many Christians expect a millennium of God's rule on Earth, an idea which corresponds closely with the thousand year Golden Age which the New Age promises.

If the idea of the New Age was expressed unclearly, people took from it what they wanted, to justify doing what they felt impelled to do. There was a growing hunger for more substantial spiritual nourishment than was offered by the mainline Christian churches and a search for other means of spiritual fulfilment. This hunger gave the opportunity for many "gurus" to arise and mislead many people. Others turned to drugs, sex, occultism and meditation and various forms of "transpersonal psychology".

The Drug Culture

In the 1960's, when the idea of the New Age and the possibility of spiritual enlightenment started to capture popular imagination, many people sought instant salvation through taking drugs, particularly the hallucinogenic drugs such as LSD or mescaline, which were legal at the time. There was an awareness that barriers exist between our ordinary consciousness and higher states. Mystical experiences were valued for their own sake and taking chemicals seemed the easiest route to cosmic consciousness.

The experience of those trying this chemical path to liberation was that, as reported by Aldous Huxley (*The Doors of Perception* and *Heaven and Hell*), the experience resulting from turning the light of consciousness in upon the mind, depends entirely upon the nature of the individual. The person of loving and gentle disposition is more likely to find incredible bliss, while the person with a heart full of evil is more likely to find the horrors of Hell.

It appears that the barriers within the mind which prevent us seeing ourselves as we are, have a real purpose in protecting our sanity until we are ready to experience higher consciousness. The drug experience drove some people to insanity which led to such drugs being declared illegal. It is clear from the teachings of spiritual masters, including Sathya Sai Baba, that liberation is not to be found in chemicals.

The Revolution in Values

Young people of the time readily took to the notion of a bright new world in the process of emergence. At a time when the world seemed under the real threat of nuclear annihilation, the old ways of their forefathers seemed anachronistic and irrelevant.

The education system of the time encouraged free-thinking on the part of students, questioning of traditional ideas and a more liberal approach to morality. Traditional means of discipline were discarded as too repressive. At the same time education became more focussed upon vocational needs rather than the development of character and learning for its own sake. Strong opposition towards any kind of spiritual or moral instruction led to the abandonment of the teaching of religious principles in publicly-owned schools.

Changes in the education system encouraged children to take nothing on trust, to question everything, including the authority of their parents. Television programmes subtly undermined respect for parents, particularly fathers, who were often portrayed as well-meaning but ineffectual wimps. Many parents were reluctant or unable to assert their authority in regulating the behaviour of their children.

With the widespread attack upon traditional moral values it is possible to make a case that there was a concerted conspiracy by many people to destroy the moral fabric of traditional Western society.

Interest in Spirituality

There was, at the time, a flowering of interest in spirituality and a turning to Eastern ideas, as well as some of the less mainstream Western ideas such as occultism and witchcraft. The idea of finding a personal "guru" became popular with such seekers, and naturally many figures arose to claim the status of guru. Inevitably, many of these self-appointed gurus turned out to be interested only in their own ego-gratification from encouraging dependence on themselves, or financial enrichment through their gullible devotees. Many people, particularly the young, followed such leaders with more enthusiasm than discrimination. Many self-styled gurus were positively evil, and were motivated by lust for power, drugs and sexual control over their followers.

Despite the spiritual hunger, Christianity, particularly as exemplified in the established churches, was not widely accepted as the answer to spiritual needs, and thus a large number of spiritual seekers felt compelled to find their own path to Salvation. Many church leaders have noted that their spiritual offerings were not seen by everyone to be the answer to the growing spiritual thirst and have tried to adapt accordingly, with rather mixed results.

Zen Buddhism achieved a level of popularity with many sectors of society, particularly those looking for a spiritual path other than Christianity as it offered a philosophy which was compatible with Christian ideals without the trappings of formal religion.

Transcendental Meditation became popular as a path to quick spiritual realisation, but offered more than it could actually deliver. Other people tried the road of throwing away **all** rules, restrictions and moral codes, thus sowing the seeds of the breakdown in the social fabric which presently threatens to overtake us all.

In the 1960's the catchcry of "If it feels good, do it" led to sex without restraint or responsibility, and a search for hedonistic satisfaction which eventually led to abuse of children and others, mainly women. Many parents of the era abandoned their responsibilities for their children, both in terms of physical support and moral guidance. Those who were children in the 1960's are the parents of the 1990's, many of whom are now raising children without clear moral standards or discipline. The results are apparent in the breakdown in codes of behaviour, morality and the general selfishness which is all too prevalent in society.

The movement which started with high-minded notions of freedom and liberality, has actually led to the bondage of many young people to drugs and other forms of vice, as well as being victims of child abuse and incest. The idea that the "New Age" meant liberation of the **flesh** to indulge itself in worldly pleasures, was a mistaken notion with tragic results. The Golden Age is liberation of the **spirit** from *"the world, the flesh and the Devil"*.

Many of the social ills of the 1990's have their roots in the 1960's.

Human Potential Movement

Another strong movement of the 1960's was the Human Potential Movement, attempting to facilitate the growth of the latent qualities of the human race, particularly spirituality. The leading light of the time was Abraham Maslow, who suggested that "Self-Actualization" became a pressing human need and occurred when all other needs (in a hierarchy of survival physical, emotional and social) were satisfied. At least Maslow may be credited with a movement to introduce spiritual values into psychology at a time when psychology would not even recognise the idea of "mind" as having any meaning.

The Human Potential Movement led to a variety of experimentation, where some people obtained some dramatic spiritual insights; while others became addicted to endless and repetitive explorations of their own psyches. The difference appeared to lie in whether they saw the ego as their ultimate self or could see beyond ego to higher levels of spirituality.

The greatest failing of the Human Potential Movement was to view Man as a biological entity rather than a Spiritual Being, and thus assume that spirituality is a luxury once all other needs are met. This is contrary to the teachings of Christ, who said:

> *"But strive first for the Kingdom of God and his righteousness, and all these things will be given to you as well."* (Matthew 6 : 33)

Many of those who identified with the New Age found themselves in trouble with the law for abusing alcohol, drugs, children or other people. Others experimented with various kinds of witchcraft or demonic cults, to the detriment of their mental, physical and spiritual health.

"New Age" Acquires Negative Associations

With such beginnings, it is no wonder that the term "New Age" has acquired a connotation as a kind of waffly mysticism bordering on the demonic, and is generally rejected by Christians.

However, if the assertions of astrologers are correct, then we can no more avoid entering the New Age of Aquarius than we can avoid entering a New Year once 31 December is past. If the term "New Age" now has a pejorative meaning, this has come from those who have abused the term for selfish ends rather than because the idea itself is evil.

Christians often feel threatened by the term for reasons they may not be able to define. Those Christians who can define their unease are responding to the belief spoken by some "New Agers" that the New Age supersedes Christianity, which belongs to a bygone era. As I will attempt to demonstrate, the opposite case applies, that Christianity will blossom in its fullness, will shine with renewed lustre in this New Golden Age.

The Golden Age is the time when the Gospel of Christ will truly be preached to all the nations, as Jesus commanded. It is the time when many of the prophecies of Jesus and the Book of Revelation will be fulfilled.

The "New Age" in the Bible

While Biblical scholars reach agreement on very few points, they do agree that one of the reasons why the Gospels were not written until more than a half-century after the crucifixion of Jesus was that they expected the return of the Lord to be any time. Jesus had often spoken of the end-times, but clearly his disciples had not understood what he was saying. In their lack of understanding, they had misinterpreted his words and created a theology of apocalypses which has been with the church ever since.

There are many references in the Bible to references to "the end of the age", "end of the world" or "end of time". The Greek word which is often translated into "age", world" or "time" is *aion,* from which we derive the English word "aeon", meaning age, or long period of time. It can be rightly said that the coming of Jesus was a new age, during which the world experienced a great change in the consciousness of its people.

Jesus often referred to the age in which He lived as coming to an end at some time, but gave few clues as to when that would be. Such clues have been subject to many interpretations. The New English Bible gives a closer and clearer translation than other versions in recounting one of Jesus' statements on the end of the age:

"When he was sitting on the Mount of Olives the disciples came to speak to him privately. 'Tell us,' they said, 'when will this happen? And what will be the signal for your coming and the <u>end of the age?</u>'"

"Jesus replied: 'Take care that no one misleads you. For many will come claiming my name and saying, "I am the Messiah"; and many will be misled by them. The time is coming when you will hear the noise of battle near at hand and the news of battles far away; see that you are not alarmed. Such things are bound to happen; but the end is still to come. For nation will make war upon nation, kingdom upon kingdom; there will be famines and earthquakes in many places. With all these things the birth-pangs of the <u>new age</u> begin.

"You will then be handed over for punishment and execution; and men of all nations will hate you for your allegiance to me. Many will lose their faith; they will betray one another and hate one another. Many false prophets will arise, and will mislead many; and as lawlessness spreads, men's love for one another will grow cold. But the man who holds out to the end will be saved. And this gospel of the Kingdom will be proclaimed throughout the earth as a testimony to all nations; and then the end will come." (New English Bible, Matthew 24 : 3-14)

Many Christians, who have taken the meaning of such texts as meaning the end of the world, have constructed a fabric of theory around what is known as the "end-times", expecting a catastrophic battle which will end civilisation as we know it. If we relate these prophecies to the end of an age, or era, then the prophecies of Jesus are more sensible and comprehensible.

The condition of the times described by Jesus in this passage relate very well to the present time in which we live, and this relationship has led many Christians to assume that we are living in the end-end-time. It can be argued that the entire mission of Jesus was concerned with the end of the current age of the world. He said:

> *"Do not think that I have come to bring peace to the earth; I have not come to bring peace, but a sword. For I have come to set a man against his father, and a daughter against her mother, and a daughter-in-law against her mother-in-law; and one's foes will be members of one's own household."* (Matthew 10 : 34-36)

When these verses are taken together with the previous passage quoted above, it could be seen that Jesus was sent to bring about the end of the age. This is in concord with Hindu scholars who say that Jesus was sent by God to hasten the end of what they call the *Kaliyuga* (the age of destruction) as a mercy to suffering humanity.

Because few people have understood the significance of the Golden Age, there are many myths and wild theories bordering at one end on a scenario which would make "Star Wars" seem tame, having Christ riding through the air on a white horse waving a sword and surrounded by hordes of angels; with another scenario popularised by the hippie movement which suggested that the Golden Age meant the freedom to live in a pleasant, drug-induced version of Heaven.

When prophecies regarding the Golden Age are properly understood as meaning a Golden Age, all humanity, including Christians should welcome it.

The Need to Discriminate

The challenge for the genuine spiritual aspirant at the present time is to recognise which aspects of the Golden Age are genuinely of God, and which have less savoury, or even demonic origins. As Jesus said:

> *"Beware of false prophets, who come to you in sheep's cloth-*
> *ing, but inwardly are ravenous wolves. You will know them*
> *by their fruits. Are grapes gathered from thorns or figs from*
> *thistles? In the same way, every good tree bears good fruit but*
> *the bad tree bears bad fruit. A good tree cannot bear bad fruit*
> *nor can a bad tree bear good fruit."* (Matthew 7 : 15-19)

God gave us discrimination to guide us and to know which prophets are true and which false. Jesus gives us a simple test which involves looking at the results of a prophets' influence. We should reject
a prophet whose fruits are bad and be prepared to accept one whose
fruits are truly of the Spirit. These good fruits are:

> *". . . love, joy, peace, patience, kindness, generosity, faithful-*
> *ness, gentleness and self-control . . ."* (Galatians 5 : 22, 23)

In their purest forms, these are the qualities which are exemplified in
the conduct of Sathya Sai Baba and pervade His teachings. Those of
His devotees who live by His teachings exude these good fruits. These
qualities will come to fruition in humanity generally in the Golden Age.

While most of us who read newspapers, watch violence and destruction on television and encounter people who live in fear, misery and
wretchedness, may think that the good fruits are largely absent from
the world, yet we have the promise of God that these things will not
always be so. The Book of Revelation promises us a thousand year
reign of God on Earth in which we will know peace, righteousness,
truth and great joy.

Jesus told us that the troubles we are now experiencing are but the
birth pangs of the new era. The darkness which we now see is but the
period before the dawn. Those who raise their eyes to the sky will see
that, even now, the first light of dawn is with us.

Sathya Sai Baba says:

> *"A revolution - more powerful and more pervasive than any*
> *that Man has undergone so far - neither political, economic,*

scientific nor technological, but deeper and more basic, is now on. It is the spiritual revolution.

"This revolution has Love as both its means and its end. It will awaken the springs of love all over the world in the fields of education, morality, law, politics, commerce and science. It will inspire man to loving service, revealing the brotherhood of man and the fatherhood of God.

"Everyone, wherever he lives, whatever his status and whichever his faith, can share in this revolution and be an instrument for the liberation of mankind from its own ignorance.

"The spiritual revolution will sharpen the inner vision of Man so that he can see his own reality. Its impact will envelop and enrich all human communities and transform mankind into a stream of willing helpers, flowing smoothly to the limitless sea of Divinity. Many hesitate to believe that things will improve, that life for all will be happy and full of joy, that the Golden Age will ever recur. Let me assure you that this Avatar has not come in vain and will succeed in averting the crisis that has come upon humanity."

View of the Sathya Sai Super Speciality Hospital

Its architect, Dr. Keith Critchlow of the Prince of Wales College of Architecture, has explained that the central dome symbolises the human heart but turned upwards towards God. The wards at the side are wrapped round like embracing arms that come round to cure and heal

The entrance lobby to the Sathya Sai Super Speciality Hospital

Featured throughout the Hospital are motifs representing the major religions of the world.

CHAPTER THREE

EARLY LIFE OF SATHYA SAI BABA

"The Roman rulers were told that Jesus was attempting to assert Himself as King and so could be punished for treason. Their insistence made the Governor order the Crucifixion. When the nails were being driven through Him on the Cross, Jesus heard the voice of the Father saying, 'All life is One, My dear Son; be alike to everyone' and Jesus pleaded that those who were crucifying Him may be pardoned, for they knew not what they did Jesus sacrificed Himself for the sake of mankind"

Sathya Sai Baba

When Christians hear of a man who has raised the dead; constantly heals the sick; can appear in different places at the same time; demonstrates knowledge of the inner secrets of all people; can speak all tongues on Earth without having studied languages; quotes from all Scriptures of the world without having read them; multiplies food to feed crowds; turns water into petrol; can appear in more than one place at a time and produces things out of the air, they should pay attention. All the known miracles demonstrated by Jesus, along with many others, have been produced by Sathya Sai Baba. There are many other parallels between the lives of Sathya Sai Baba and Jesus in man other ways.

In Sanscrit Jesus is written as "Isa", with the "I" meaning "mother" and the "Sa" meaning "Divine". The name of Jesus therefore means "Divine Mother", which describes the loving, caring concern which Jesus has for suffering humanity. The same component sounds may be also written as "Sai" to have the same meaning. This is, of course, part of the name of Sathya Sai Baba.

The most authoritative biographer of Sathya Sai Baba is His long-time devotee, Professor N Kasturi, for whom we are indebted for many writings about Swami. Professor Kasturi was himself a most remarkable man with a keen mind and an enquiring nature. He could not be described as gullible or easily misled. He may be regarded as a reliable reporter and witness. The following details are summarized from various of his works.

Conception

Sathya Sai Baba was born in the village of Puttaparthi, Andhra Pradesh, Southern India on 23 November 1926, the third child of Pedda Venkappa Raju and Easwaramma. The manner of the conception of Sathya Sai Baba also parallels that of Jesus. From Matthew 1 : 18-25 we read:

> *"Now the birth of Jesus the Messiah took place in this way. When his mother Mary had been engaged to Joseph, but before they lived together, she was found to be with child from the Holy Spirit. Her husband Joseph, being a righteous man and unwilling to expose her to public disgrace, planned to dismiss her quietly. But just when he had resolved to do this, an angel of the Lord appeared to him in a dream and said, "Joseph, son of David, do not be afraid to take Mary as your wife, for the child conceived in her is from the Holy Spirit. She will bear a*

son, and you are to name him Jesus, for he will save his people from their sins." All this took place to fulfil what had been spoken by the Lord through the prophet:

'Look, the virgin shall conceive and bear a son, and they shall name him Emmanuel,' which means, 'God is with us.'

When Joseph awoke from sleep, he did as the angel of the Lord commanded him; he took her as his wife, but had no marital relations with her until she had borne a son; and he named him Jesus."

An account of the conception of Sathya Sai Baba is given by his mother, Easwaramma in the following story:

"As Baba sat one day surrounded by His devotees, there was an abrupt interruption. A pundit, Mr. Rama Sarma, well versed in the holy Puranas, felt a sudden urge to ask a question. "Swami! Was your incarnation a Pravesa (an Entrance) or a Prasava (natural conception)?" Baba turned to his Mother to answer the question. His Mother said "I had dreamt of Satyanarayana Deva (an angel of God) and he cautioned me that I should not be frightened if something happens to me through the Will of God. That morning, when I was at the well drawing water, a big ball of blue light came rolling towards me and I fainted and fell. I felt it glide into me.

"Baba turned to Rama Sarma with a smile. 'There, you have the answer! I was not begotten. It was Pravesa, not Prasava.'" (from "Easwaramma", ch 2, by N. Kasturi)

Birth of Sathya Sai Baba

During the pregnancy of Easwaramma the Raju household became accustomed to strange events in the household. At night musical instruments would play on their own. The events are rather beautifully described by Prof Kasturi:

"The material sheath which the Lord once again willed to wear was formed; It grew from week to week. Mysterious intimations of the impending incarnation disturbed the even tenor of Pedda Venkapa's family life! For example there was the twang of the tambura ! Since the brothers and the father were all very much interested in the village operas on Puranic incidents and since one play or other was always being rehearsed at home, there was substantially big tambura, leaning against the wall and a 'Maddala' or drum on the floor beneath. These two were silent only when the inmates of the house retired for the night. But as the birth of the son for whom Sri Easwaramma prayed, announced itself as imminent, the house was awakened at midnight, and sometime even later, by the tambura twanging automatically and the maddala, beating rhythmically as if an expert Hand was handling it! Various theories were promulgated to explain this phenomenon by the wise men of the village but, since they only added to the mystery Pedda Venkapa Raju hurried to Bukkapatnam where there was a Sastri, on whose interpretation he could place faith. The Sastri said that it was an auspicious occurrence; it meant the presence of a Sakthi. a beneficent Power, conferring Harmony Melody. Order Symmetry, Spiritual Elevation and Joy. " - From Sathyam, Sivam, Sundarum, Vol 1 p 7,8

Childhood

It was apparent to all who knew Him, that the young Sathyanarayana was a special child. He was known to be totally honest and would readily admit any mistakes. Kasturi writes:

"He kept away from places where pigs or sheep or cattle or fowl, were killed or tortured, or where fish were trapped or caught. when a bird was selected and talked about by someone in connection with dinner, Satyanarayana the little boy would run towards it and clasp it to His bosom and fondle it as if the

extra love He poured on it would induce the elders to relent and spare the fowl.

He rarely retaliated when He was handled roughly by play-mates; information of such ill-treatment came to the parents through other toddlers who witnessed the affair, never from Sathya, who seemed not in the least to suffer pain or discomfiture." - ibid, p 10

Early Miracles

During childhood, Sathya used to delight in playing tricks with and for his friends. He had a "magic bag" out of which came an apparently endless supply of sweets and other good things for the other children. He was given to multiplying food while still a child. Kasturi tells of one witness:

"Very often, when the food cooked threatened to be too small in quantity, Baba was quietly informed and in the words of an old lady, 'He asked two coconuts to be brought; when they were given to Him, He struck one against the other and both broke exactly into halves; He then sprinkled the coconut water on the little heaps of rice and the vessels containing the other items, and gave us the signal to proceed with the task of serving all who have come or may come, until dusk!'" - ibid p 45.

Another well-known miracle of the young Swami's is known as "the wish-fulfilling tree", a tamarind tree on the crest of a hill overlooking the Chittravathi river. He used to take His friends to the top and take various varieties of fruits, including apples, mangoes, oranges and figs.

Kasturi writes of these games around the hill:

"He got up the rocks quick and fast, to the surprise of everyone; indeed, sometimes He did not even climb at all; still, He would be talking to the devotees on the sands one moment and

hail them from near the tamarind tree, the next. He usually help up the older and the fatter among the devotees and when they held His hand, He pulled them up as if they had no weight at all." - ibid, p48

Announcement to his family

Prof Kasturi writes in his biography on the earlier years of Sathya Sai Baba (Sathyam Sivam Sundaram) the following account of the announcement of His mission:

"One could sense that Sathyanarayana was getting more and more reluctant to be bound by routine; he was tugging at the bonds, for History was whispering in His ear, to break away and reach out to the four quarters! The period of probation which Sai Baba had allotted to the people around Him was over; He saw that the moment had come to emerge, to be always Sai for every one.

"On the 20th day of October, 1940, the day after they all returned from Hampi by special bus, Sathyanarayana started for school as usual. The Excise Inspector of the place, Sri Anjaneyulu who was very much attached to the little Baba, accompanied Him, as far as the school gate and went home, rather reluctantly. He seemed to see a superb halo, round the face of Baba that day and he could not take his eyes away from that enchantment.

Within a few minutes, Baba too turned back to the house. Standing on the outer doorstep, he cast aside the books He was carrying and called out, "I am no longer your Sathya." "I am Sai." The sister-in-law came from the kitchen and peeped out; she was almost blinded by the splendour of the halo, which she saw around Baba's head! She closed her eyes and shrieked. Baba addressed her, "I am going; I don't belong to you Maya (worldly illusion) has gone; My Bhakthas are calling me; I have My Work. I can't stay any longer."

And, so saying, He turned back and left in spite of her plead-ings. The brother hurried home on hearing all this; but, Baba only told him, "Give up all your efforts to 'cure' Me; I am Sai; I do not consider Myself related to you." Neighbour Sri Narayana Sastri heard the noise; he listened and realised that it was something serious; he ran in; he saw the splendour of the 'halo' and fell at Baba's feet. He too heard the Historic Declaration, "Maya (Worldly illusion) has left; I am going; My work is waiting." - ibid p 38

An incident a little later is worth noting:

"Some one challenged Sathyanarayana and asked Him, 'If you are Sai Baba, show us some proof, now!" Baba replied, 'Yes, I shall and everyone came nearer. 'Place in my hand those jasmine flowers,' He commanded. It was done. With a quick gesture, He threw them on the floor and said 'Look.' They saw that the flowers had formed, while falling, the Telugu letters, Sai Baba! - ibid, p 39.

The Sai Mission

The mission of Sathya Sai Baba starts with nothing less than the refor-mation of the character of Man, which is much the same as the mission of Jesus except that the danger which Man has to be rescued from is so much more acute and the evil over the Earth is so much greater. He says:

"Your innate laziness prevents you from the spiritual exercise necessary to understand God. This laziness should go. It has to be driven out of man's nature in whatever shape it appears. This is My mission. My task is not merely to cure and console and remove individual misery. It is something far more impor-tant. The removal of misery and distress is incidental to My mission."

"My main task is the re-establishment of the sacred scriptures and revealing knowledge of them to all peoples. This task will succeed. It will not be limited. It will not be slowed down.

When the Lord decides and wills, His Divine Will cannot be hindered."

Sathya Sai Baba's mission is to save all mankind by restoring Love, Truth, Peace and Righteousness. His statement of His mission echos that of the *Bhagavad Gita,* the great Holy Scripture of India:

"For the protection of the virtuous, for the destruction of evil and for establishing righteousness on a firm footing, I incarnate from age to age. Whenever ashanti (discord, restlessness) overwhelms the world, the Lord will incarnate in human form to establish the modes of earning prashanti (supra-peace) and to re-educate the human community in the ways of peace.

"At the present time, strife and discord have robbed peace and unity from the family, the school, the community, society, villages and the state. The arrival of the Lord is anxiously awaited by sages and saints. Saints have prayed and I have come. My main tasks are fostering the scriptures and fostering of devotees. Your virtue, your self-control, your faith, your steadfastness - these are the signs by which people read of my Glory.

"You can lay claim to be my devotee only when you have placed yourself in My hands fully and completely, with no trace of ego. You can enjoy the bliss through the experience which the Avatar confers. The Avatar behaves in a human way so that mankind may feel kinship, but rises to superhuman heights so that mankind may aspire to reach the heights and, through that aspiration, can actually reach Him.

"Realizing the Lord within you as the motivator is the task for which He comes in human form. Avataras like Rama and Krishna had to kill one or more individuals who could be identified as enemies of the dharmic (righteous) way of life and thus restore the practice of virtue. But now, there is no-one fully good. And so who deserves the protection of God? All are

tainted by wickedness, and so who will survive if the Avatara decides to uproot wickedness?

One of the most beautiful summaries of Sathya Sai Baba's mission is expressed by Himself in the following words:

"I have come to light the lamp of love in your hearts, to see that it shines day by day with added lustre. I have not come to speak on behalf of any teaching, like the Hindu teaching. I have not come on any mission of publicity for any sect or creed or cause; nor have I come to collect the followers for any doctrine. I have no plan to attract disciples or devotees into my fold or any fold. I have come to tell you of this unitary faith, this Atmic principle, this path of love, this duty to love, this obligation to love."

In other discourses He indicates that the establishment of spiritual values is only the beginning of His mission. The human race has reached the stage in its evolution in which many more people are ready to realise their Divinity and return to God in spiritual form in the same way as Jesus did. As it says in John 1 : 9-12:

"The true light, which enlightens everyone was coming into the world . . . . But to all who received him, who believed in his name he gave power to become children of God, who were born, not of blood or of the will of the flesh or of the will of man, but of God"

Some students of spirituality have remarked that after the time of Jesus, there was an increase in the level of consciousness of the human race, with more intelligence and understanding of the laws of Nature. We can expect a further increase in human consciousness as a result of the Advent of Sathya Sai Baba.

It is our destiny develop God-consciousness and thus complete the cycle of evolution. It represents nothing less than a massive leap in the evolution of the human race. This is what Sathya Sai Baba has come to facilitate and to enlist our help in achieving. We are called to join in nothing less than a great leap in the spiritual evolution of Mankind. This is truly a breathtaking idea!

Publicizing Sathya Sai Baba

Sathya Sai Baba avoids publicity for Himself. Indeed, it appears to be one of His miracles that, despite the large numbers of people who claim to be devotees (in excess of 70 million, with one estimate of 140 million), comparatively few people know of Him. There have been journalists who have written sensational articles which they find no editor will publish, and others who prepare television documentaries which arouse surprisingly little interest. Sathya Sai Baba Himself says:

> *"The Lord has no intention to publicize Himself. I do not need publicity, nor does any other avatara of the Lord. What are you daring to publicize? -- Me? What do you know about Me? You say one thing about Me today and another thing tomorrow. Your faith has not become unshakeable. You praise Me when things go well and blame Me when things go wrong. When you start publicity you descend to the level of all those who compete in collecting money by decrying others and extolling themselves."*

> *"Only inferior minds will revel in publicity and self-aggrandizement. These have no relevance in the case of avataras; they need no advertisement."*

He also makes the point that He is not after converts for the Name and Form of Sathya Sai Baba. He says:

> *"I do not mention Sai Baba in any of My discourses. Though I bear the name Avatara of Sai Baba, I do not appreciate in the least the distinctions between the various aspects of God -- Sai, Rama, Krishna and others. I do not proclaim that this one is more important or that is less important.*

"Continue the worship of your chosen God along the lines already familiar to you. Then you will find that you are coming nearer and nearer to Me. For all names are Mine and all forms are Mine.

"There is no need to change your chosen God and adopt a new one when you have seen Me and heard Me."

Sathya Sai Baba makes the point in various ways that the only reason God incarnates on Earth is for the good of Mankind. He obtains no joy or satisfaction for Himself. The purpose of His coming is stated thus:

"Every step in the life of the Avatara is predetermined. Rama came to feed the roots of Sathya (Truth) and Dharma (Righteousness). Krishna came to foster Shanti (Peace) and Prema (Love). Now all these four are running dry. That is why the present Avatara has come. The dharma that has fled to the forests has to be led back to the villages and towns. The anti-dharma that is ruining the villages and towns has to driven back into the jungle."

"I have come to give you the key to the treasure of ananda (bliss), to tell you how to tap that spring, for you have forgotten the way to blessedness. If you waste this chance of saving yourself, it is just your fate. You have come to get from Me tinsel and trash, the petty little cures and promotions, worldly jobs and comforts. Very few have come to get from Me the thing I have come to give you, namely, liberation itself. Even among those few who stick to the path of spiritual endeavour, those who succeed are a handful."

Nearly two thousand years ago, Jesus said:

"Not everyone who says unto me, Lord, Lord' will enter the Kingdom of heaven, but only the one who does the will of my Father in heaven." (Matthew 7 : 21)

Echoing those words of Jesus, Baba says:

> *"Where money is calculated, gathered or exhibited to demonstrate one's achievements, I will not be present. I come only where sincerity of faith and surrender (to the will of God) are valued."*

One of most amazing statements (to my own mind) which Baba has made is that nobody can dream of Him unless He wills it. Every dream involving Him, contains a message from Him. The truth of this statement is borne out by countless testimonies of devotees.

The Sathya Sai Baba Social Revolution

Sathya Sai Baba has undertaken the practical task of reforming the world through reform of social services, starting with education and health. His agenda is foreshadowed in His statement that there are three things which should be free of cost as of right to all people. These are Education, Health and Food. He is currently focussing on the first two of this triad, and has started pilot schemes for the provision of free food in at least two villages in India.

Education was the first area of His attention as the future of the race depends upon the development of leaders endowed with spiritual values. Swami has endowed schools and colleges in every state of India, from primary level to post-graduate universities. Sathya Sai schools are also taking root in other countries and should soon be established world-wide. In all these institutions, spiritual values are taught as fundamental along with traditional curriculae.

Health is being reformed through the establishment of "Super Speciality" hospitals. The first hospital has been established at Prasanthi Nilayam and when completed will concentrate on treating diseases of the heart, liver, lungs and kidneys. The hospital is open to patients from all countries, all treatment is free of cost to the patient. Some of the world's leading surgeons and medical workers are attracted to work in the hospital without payment as an act of spiritual service. The spiritual emphasis in the hospital aims to heal the whole person rather than just treat the physical disease. Patients and staff all benefit from being in that Holy Place.

The construction of the hospital is marvellous story. The first wing was constructed in ten months from first plans to first operation. The construction phase itself took only five months, though the "experts" had said that it could not be completed within five years! Those involved agree that it was only the influence of Swami which led to the apparently miraculously short construction time.

Sathya Sai Baba states that this hospital will set the standards for medical care in India and the world for the next thousand years. Thus the Golden Age of Medicine is evolving within our sight in Prasanthi Nilayam.

Sathya Sai Baba is involved in a re-afforestation program within India. He teaches that climatic changes in the world are the direct result of Man's interference with Nature, particularly in the felling of forests and greater emissions of carbon dioxide. Much of India is now denuded of the forests which used to cover the land, and the land has turned to desert. A program under His inspiration uses Australian trees to provide cover for the growth of indigenous Indian trees, with the intention of returning the desert areas to productive uses.

Use of Human Agents

While there are miraculous aspects to the work of Sathya Sai Baba, it is notable that He uses human agents wherever possible. He takes a direct interest in the design and construction of buildings and institutions which bear His name. He is the source of inspiration either directly or indirectly for all major projects. At the opening of the Super Specialty Hospital He commented that He could have waved His hand and manifested the building (and most of His devotees have no doubt that he could do exactly that, if He chose); He commented that such an action is not appropriate in the current age. Human architects, builders and labourers constructed the physical building, but nobody has any doubts as to the source of inspiration.

He makes it very clear that He has not come to undertake all the work Himself, but to enlist our aid in the spiritual revolution. When John Hislop once addressed Sathya Sai Baba and referred to "your mission" he was corrected and reminded that the work is "our mission". He has called certain individuals to help in furthering the mission around the world. It will not be long before everyone is called upon to help.

There are many social service projects around the world conducted under the auspices of the Sathya Sai movement. In India, there are large-scale projects to feed the hungry, help the poor and relieve misery. In New Zealand, Sathya Sai devotees work with The Salvation Army in distribution of food parcels and providing meals to the elderly. Medical clinics providing free medical checkups to those who cannot afford doctors are provided in many places. The scope of Sathya Sai service activities is already vast throughout the world and is growing at a very fast rate. This work is motivated by love for Sathya Sai Baba, and Swami's statement that "Service to Man is service to God."

Understanding Sathya Sai Baba

The more one tries to understand Sathya Sai Baba, the more of a mystery He becomes. In His presence one becomes aware that here is a Being who knows literally whenever the wind blows through a blade of grass, who knows our every thought, word and action. He is also involved constantly in keeping the whole Universe functioning, at every level from the smallest atomic particle to the biggest constellation of stars. Not only does He know all these things in the present, but He is conscious of the infinite past and the infinite future at the same time. He says:

"Your worldly intelligence cannot fathom the ways of God. He cannot be recognised by mere cleverness or intelligence. You may benefit from God, but you cannot explain Him. Your explanations are only conjecture, attempts to cloak your ignorance in pompous expressions. Bring something into your daily practice as evidence of your having known the secret of Higher Life from Me. Show that you have greater brotherliness, speak

with more sweetness and self-control. Bear defeat as well as victory with calm resignation."

"I am always aware of the future, the past as well as the present of each one of you, so I am not so moved by mercy. Since I know the past, the background, the reaction is different. It is the consequence of evil deliberately done in the past birth and so I allow your suffering to continue, often modified with some small compensation. I do not cause grief or joy; you are the designer of both these chains which bind you."

Baba makes the point time and again that He cannot be understood by intellectual analysis, but by absorbing Him and His message into the heart.

Sathya Sai Baba attracts our attention with what we call His miracles, but he takes pains to point out that they are only His playfulness. He often describes them as His "calling cards" to demonstrate that He is not like other people.

"My acts are the foundation on which I am building my work -- the task for which I have come. All the miracles which you observe are to be interpreted so. The foundation for a dam requires the right materials; without them it will not last and hold back the waters."

Sense of Urgency

Many a time Sathya Sai Baba mentions the need for urgency in the spiritual conversion of people. Life is short enough He declares, and the purpose of our existence is to become one with God. We should utilise our every moment for that end. All we have in life is time and Baba often says *"Time waste is life waste"*, or *"Time is God, do not waste time."*

It is out of ignorance that we become diverted into time-wasting activities, many of which take us away from spirituality and into inevitable misery. We depart from spirituality when our hearts become attached to the things of this world, to possessions, to status, to our jobs and our relationships. Baba does not tell us to renounce these things, or to avoid responsibilities. He does tell us not to bind ourselves to them so that they take over our lives.

> *"Practice detachment from now on; practice it little by little, for a day will come sooner or later when you will have to give up all you hold dear. Do not go on adding to the things which bind you to them. Bind yourself to the great liberator, God."*

The New Jerusalem

Sathya Sai Baba established the base of His ministry by building an ashram on the outskirts of His birthplace in Puttaparthi. The name for the ashram is Prasanthi Nilayam ("the Abode of Eternal Peace").

"Jerusalem" is sometimes called *the city of Everlasting Peace*. Many Jewish and Christian mystical writings have spoken of the new Jerusalem as being the centre of God's work on Earth for the Golden Millennium. Prophets have spoken of the significance of Jerusalem as a sign of the fulfilment of God's promises to establish His reign. It is worth asking the question as to whether the "new Jerusalem" is in fact now called "Prashanti Nilayam"-- in other words, the name and description of God's seat of government is correct, but the words need translation from Hebrew to Sanskrit.

Swami has said that in time to come, Prashanti Nilayam will be bigger and more significant than Delhi. The rate of building which is occurring at present in Puttaparthi and the ashram area, and the accelerating pace of His mission, makes this claim most credible.

The Essential Message

Sathya Sai Baba teaches that all people are of the one source and have a common destiny. Differences between people are based upon faulty thinking and the delusions of the ego. When we see the Truth for what it is, then these differences cease to divide us. It will happen that when every person understands this Truth, that harmony will be restored on the Earth, and humanity attain the realization of its destiny.

Sathya Sai Baba says:

"All religions teach one basic discipline; the removal from the mind of the blemish of egoism of running after little joys. Every religion teaches man to fill his being with the glory of God and evict the pettiness of conceit. It trains him in the methods of detachment and discrimination so that he may aim high and attain liberation.

"Believe that all hearts are motivated by the One and Only God; that all faiths glorify the One and Only God; that all Names in all languages and all forms man can conceive denote the One and Only God. Cultivate the attitude of Oneness between people of all creeds, all countries and all continents. This is the message of love I bring. That is the message I wish you to take to heart."

Sathya Sai Baba

The Sathya Sai Institute of Higher Learning (university) at Puttaparthi

The Planetarium, part of the University Campus at Puttaparthi

It is equipped with a Spitz Space System providing a star-field of 4054 images, including 88 recognised constellations and 57 navigational stars. The tilted hyposphere permits unidirectional viewing.

CHAPTER FOUR

SATHYA SAI BABA ON JESUS

Jesus was compassion come in human form. He spread the spirit of compassion and conferred solace on the distressed and the suffering. good works always provoke the wicked, but one should not falter or fear when opposition obstructs. Jesus was the target for many mighty obstacles and He braved them all. As a result, His Name, story and message are still shedding splendorous light all over the world

Sathya Sai Baba

Sathya Sai Baba reinforces the main teachings from all the major religions of the world. However, it is clear from the number of references to Jesus in His discourses and the special nature of Christmas celebrations in Prashanti Nilayam that there is a close link between Jesus Christ and Sathya Sai Baba. Sathya Sai Baba reinforces the main teachings of Jesus at the same time as He adds new meanings and presents them in a more modern idiom. He takes nothing away from the Gospel of Jesus, but adds considerably to our understanding of Him.

Every Christmas Baba gives a special Christmas discourse where He speaks of Jesus and His life. Many facts about Jesus which had been lost are revived in these discourses. Sometimes some aspects of the teachings of Jesus are explained. In these Christmas discourses, Jesus is depicted in a way which makes Him a more credible person than the sometimes shadowy Man of the New Testament. Christians who hear these discourses come away with their faith in Christ increased, and their commitment to follow Jesus enlarged.

Sathya Sai Baba affirms the Divinity and the authenticity of Jesus. Baba does not seek followers for Himself, He is content if people live more fully the Gospel of Jesus.

The following passages are from some of the Christmas discourses.

> *"Every man has to come into the world as a Messenger of God. Jesus announced Himself as a Messenger of God. He spent many years in austerities so that He could shower compassion and love on all humanity. Later He asked Himself, 'Am I just a Messenger, or am I more closely related to God, a part of God with the Divine as my essence?' Jesus spent twelve long years, wandering alone in deserts engaged on this enquiry. At the end of this period, He returned to the society of men and announced 'I am the Son of God'.*
>
> *At that time, the priests of the holy temples of Jerusalem had become corrupt and commercialised. They had deteriorated into proud and selfish men. Jesus condemned them and tried to root out the evil practices. All forms were, in the eyes of Jesus, Divine Forms, and He could not tolerate any action which belied this status. When asked by people who he was, He could reply 'I and my Father are One.' Jesus tried to teach everyone the Fatherhood of God and the Brotherhood of Man."*

"Try to be like Jesus. Jesus was a person whose only joy was in spreading Divine Love, offering Divine Love, receiving Divine Love and Living on Divine Love.

"There are various theories about the date of birth of Jesus based on the bright star that appeared on His birth. It is visible once in 800 years, it is said. Some say that He was born on the fifteenth day of September. But He was born at 3.15 am (early morning) on December 28, 1980 years ago. It was Sunday. The star that appeared that day appears only once in 800 years. Its appearance had nothing to do with the birth of Jesus. There is no rule that when Divine Energy or Divine Incarnation descends on Earth a star has to appear. That is the opinion of devotees only. But Jesus was a Star of infinite value, spreading brilliance of infinite dimension. Why posit another less brilliant glow?" (from the Christmas Day discourse 1979)

When one sees Jesus in the light shone on Him by Sathya Sai Baba, Jesus actually is seen to be more magnificent and glorious even than traditional Christianity would have us believe.

Swami said in His Christmas discourse for 1980:

"This day, Christmas is celebrated. Bring to mind the words Jesus uttered, the advice he offered, the warnings he gave, and decide to direct your daily lives along the path Jesus laid down. His words must be imprinted on your hearts and you must resolve to practise all that he taught.

"Jesus wandered purposefully in lonely places for twelve long years, engaging himself in study, spiritual exercises and meditation on God. Of course, one must protect and preserve the body, which is a Divine gift, a boat equipped with instruments which takes man across the Sea of Perpetual Change to reach Divinity. This goal of life has to be reached before the body-boat develops leaks and disintegrates through

illness, sloth and senility. Physical, mental and spiritual health have to be fostered with vigilant care. Nevertheless, one must be ever ready to cast the body away, in defence of Dharma or Daiva (Goodness or God). Have Jesus as your ideal for this. He exhorted all to observe the basically valid teachings of the ancient scriptures and derive peace and joy therefrom.

The Jews held the rituals and regulations laid down by the prophets in the scriptural texts as valid for all time and so they held the teachings of Jesus wrong. They were not moved by personal hatred towards Jesus. This problem arises in every age - the conflict between the letter and spirit - the doctrines that are held to be holy, the various do's and don'ts that have to be scrupulously followed and the underlying Truth.

The best way to resolve the confusion and conflicts that hamper moral, ethical, material, technological and spiritual progress is for man to live as fully as man ought to, and rise to the height of the Divine, that is his Reality. That is the one eternal, universal teaching. The thoughts that the intellect frames must be reflected as feeling in the mind and translated into action by the hands. Thought, word, and deed must be coordinated. They must fulfil one another. The sign of a holy person or Mahatma, is, "Manasyekam Vachasyekam Karmanekam", "One mind, one word, one act".

"Christmas means the Mass that is held on the Birthday of Christ. It is fundamentally a sacred religious rite. To deal with it as if it is a festival for drinking and dancing or only for recalling Jesus to memory, is very wrong. The day must be spent in prayer; not merely this day, but cultivate the sadhana (spiritual discipline) of prayer as a normal way of life. Prayers for worldly ends do not reach God. They will reach only those deities who deal with such restricted spheres. But all prayers arising from pure love, unselfish eagerness to render service

and from hearts that are all inclusive will reach God. For God is the very Embodiment of Love. We know that we can see the Moon only through Moonlight. So too, God who is Love can be realised only through Love. Love is God, Live in Love. That is the Message I give you."

(From the Christmas Eve Discourse, 1980)

The image of Christ from the Shroud materialised by Baba

Two ladies sat in Darshan. One, a devout Christian, had a black-and- white computer print-out of the face of Christ from the imprint on the Shroud of Turm, and she held it out for Sai Baba to bless. Baba circled His hand above it and the picture completely disappeared, - leaving only a blank piece of paper. Then he passed His hand over it again, and this picture appeared, now in color.

CHAPTER FIVE

JESUS IN THE LIGHT OF NEW KNOWLEDGE

The Divine, though moving among all and sundry, can never be affected or deflected Envious folk heaped insults on Jesus. Even among His disciples, some betrayed Him and deserted Him. Selfish people turn envious at greatness and goodness but, since the Fure Love (Prema,) of Jesus had no trace of self in it, He was unafraid The loveless are enveloped in fear Love instils courage and promotes adventure. If you follow the Master you can face the Devil, fight to the end, and finish the game.

Sathya Sai Baba

There are many attempts in the present "rational" age to understand the significance of Jesus Christ. Theologians of various shades, certain bishops and noted clerics, as well as atheists and agnostics are seeking to redefine the traditional ideas surrounding Jesus, the question of His divinity, miracles, resurrection and actual teachings. The cross-currents of ideas reported in the news media create confusion, cynicism and doubts in even some of the most faithful of followers of Jesus. Even many of the traditional churches have been less than forthright in declaring their spiritual values. Politicians have sensed for some time that there is no political milage to be gained in defending Christian (or any) spiritual values, as the confusion has aroused the suspicion that there are no absolute Truths. When those people entrusted to represent and advocate the highest spiritual values lose faith in those values, as many have, then the decline of civilisation is inevitable. This is how the churches have, in so many cases, lost their authority to present God's message to the world.

There are systematic attempts in the current age, to "demythologise" any belief system which has elements of the supernatural. To those people who believe that the supernatural is also irrational and therefore non-sensible, there is a need to make all the ways of God comprehensible. Some theologians assert that Jesus did not actually perform the miracles recorded in the New Testament and have suggested various explanations as to how the events described may actually have happened. The motives for making such explanations is ostensibly to make Christianity more acceptable to rational thought.

Such attempts to understand God must be doomed to failure in the long run, for the simple reason that the finite mind will never understand Infinite Mind. However, those who are attempting to rationalise Christianity are making their presence felt within Christendom, in destructive ways, and have caused much confusion.

There is a school of thought which suggests that Christianity as we know it is largely a product of Paul and the Church of Rome, which may well be the actual case. In attempting to find the historical Jesus in the midst of Pauline myth, however, this school often claims that Jesus was no more than a failed political reformer who was executed after an abortive attempt at rebellion against Rome. Such a view goes much too far, and misses the whole point of Jesus' mission and significance.

In the current age it is now possible to take a fresh look at Jesus in the light of knowledge available to us through recent archeological finds and the inspiration of Sathya Sai Baba. I am convinced that such a fresh look will reveal a majesty and glory to Jesus which has been buried under rigid orthodox thinking and adherence to faulty traditions and Scriptures.

The problem for the scholar in evaluating Jesus Christ is to find:

a. Who was Jesus the man?
b. What was Jesus' mission?
c. What was Jesus' message?
d. What is the significance of Jesus for our time?

To answer these questions is beyond the scope of this book and my own knowledge. However, they can be partially answered by putting together all the pieces of knowledge that we have from all sources, many of which Christian orthodoxy has rejected in the past as not conforming to traditional wisdom. I pray that in time Sathya Sai Baba Himself will throw more light on these questions.

What is required is a scholarly effort, conducted with an open mind, to explore all available resources. There needs to be an integration of knowledge from Jewish, Roman, Syrian, Indian and Tibetan writings, not forgetting recent discoveries of the texts from Nag Hammadi as well as Qumran. The opening of the Vatican library to all scholars would be of inestimable help, as they are known to have much material denied to scholars of the world in order to maintain their hold on traditional teachings.

What needs to be avoided on the one hand, is the mind-set that the version promulgated by the Church of Rome has to be defended at all costs, and, on the other hand, that there is no such realm as the supernatural and that Jesus may be viewed purely as a social or political phenomenon.

It is also necessary, in my view, to understand Jesus in the light of the tradition of avatars. An avatar is an incarnation of God in physical form, possessing divine powers.

It is said that avatars with full or partial powers have incarnated from time to time in human history for the purpose of awakening, developing, and restoring spiritual qualities in Mankind. Christians assert that Jesus was such a being, but make the mistake of asserting that Jesus was the **only** such being despite the fact that they expect a return visit.

It is my contention that attempts to understand Jesus in isolation from other spiritual traditions will not succeed. Jesus came to earth for the benefit of all people, not just Westerners or Christians. There is evidence that his work had effects on human consciousness outside of what is normally regarded as the Christian world. Some historians have noted that humanity everywhere showed an increased level of mental functioning about this time. In some traditions, the crucifixion of Jesus took place so that He accepted the negative karma of the world, thereby removing much of the evil effects of human wrongdoing. Such a view is not at all inconsistent with the Christian assertion that Jesus gave His life for our sins.

By studying the Sai Avatar, we can understand better the workings of the Christ Avatar, who is of the same Being, in any case.

As a Christian, I used to bemoan the fact that the Bible provides only fragments of the life and teachings of Jesus, all of them precious, but obviously incomplete. Scripture raised as many questions as there were answers. I found Jesus to be a very attractive figure, but at times shadowy and insubstantial. I also found that many commentators read into the character of Jesus whatever they wanted, ranging all the way between "Gentle Jesus, meek and mild", to the angry, avenging figure who threw the money-changers out of the temple at Jerusalem.

Christians trying to fully understand Jesus had to infer what Jesus **might** have taught on various topics from His stand on other principles, but there is room for considerable dispute and disagreement between Christians.

At a time when it had been thought that no new knowledge could be discovered about a man who lived in apparent obscurity some 2,000 years ago, there are many new things we are now learning about Jesus and His times. Needless to say, the sources of information are disputed by many scholars, and there will be some debate before the new information is accepted as authentic. It is not my purpose to enter into these debates here, but the reader has many other works available to study the merits of each argument and to make up his or her own mind.

We have the unprecedented advantage in our own time to obtain authoritative teaching on the issues around Jesus directly from the Father who sent Him and declared 2,000 years ago

> *"You are my Son, the Beloved; with you I am well pleased"*
> Mark 1 : 11

When Christians ask of Sathya Sai Baba the right questions, with sincerity and faith, the Lord will provide the correct answers. What more could we ask?

A photo of Jesus, aged 29, materialised by Baba

A picture of Jesus created by Sai Baba just before Christmas 1984. After first being given to an Argentinian, Sai then donated one big one to Venezuela during the Christmas celebrations of 1987. He also allowed six copies to be made, which He then blessed and donated to various Countries around the world: Spain, Denmark, England, New Zealand, Mexico and Argentina. He also donated some small copies to Italy to be given to devotees. Baba said that this was a true likeness of Jesus and that He was 29 years old in that photo. Many 'second-generation' photos have been done from the first ones.

The 'Sarva Dharma' symbol in Prasanthi, standing for the fundamental unity of all religions

The Administration Building for all the different campuses of the Sathya Sai Institute of Higher Learning

CHAPTER SIX

THE GOSPEL OF SATHYA SAI BABA

If the name of Jesus is glorified all over the world today, it is because of His boundless Love. He served the lowly and the lost and in the end offered His life itself as a sacrifice. How many of those who call themselves devotees of Jesus, are following His teachings? 1 here are many who claim to be Sal devotees, but how many of them are /following the message of Sal? Anyone who claims to be a Sal devotee, should dedicate his life to Sal idea/s. That is true devotion and real penance. That is the hallmark of humanness. It wi/i be reflected in love, which will find expression in compassion that generates real joy (Ananda).

Sathya Sal Baba

Sathya Sai Baba has not formulated a comprehensive and systematic theology, to my knowledge. There is, however, a vast and growing collection of books and articles written by Him, and many accounts written by people who have spent a great deal of time with Him. The formulation given below is my own understanding of what a simple statement of the main messages from Baba would look like.

Sathya Sai Baba tells us:

1. We are all children of God, Divine in our own Nature and equal before God. We should therefore seek to live in unity and harmony with all peoples, irrespective of creed, color or other qualities.
2. We live in ignorance of our true Nature and purpose of our existence.
3. Our spirit has evolved from mineral existence to vegetable, animal and now as human.
4. The purpose of our existence is to realize our Divinity.
5. It is through sin (impurities in our character) that we are separated from God.
6. Until we remove the impurities, we are condemned to repeated birth on Earth.
7. By turning our lives over to God, He will purify our lives help us to manifest the Divine qualities which are ours by right.
8. When Divinity becomes manifest in us, we are saved from the need for further birth in human form.
9. All religions are paths to the same goal, they all teach the same basic morality and all adore the same God -- for there is only one God and He is omnipresent.

The broad logic of these statements will be familiar to Christians, except for the references to evolution under point 3 and reincarnation in points 5. and 7. Evolution is a doctrine which divides Christians into those who accept the findings of Science, and those who hold to a strict Creationism.

Reincarnation is likely to be seen as perhaps the most radical doctrine with which Christians may need to come to terms if they are to accept the teachings of Sathya Sai Baba, and it therefore deserves a chapter of explanation on its own. (See Chapter 10.)

1. We are all children of God, Divine in our own Nature and equal before God.

Sathya Sai Baba says that the feeling of separation of one person from another is illusory. He often likens individual consciousness to waves on the surface of the ocean. On the surface they appear different, but underneath they are all of the one substance. Their lives are short and their form changing. He says:

> *"You feel that there is something behind and beyond all this fleeting fantasy; something that persists through all the successes and defeats, all the tears and smiles, all the mirth and moan; but you are unable to grasp it and realise that it is the same entity which underlies the entire universe. You are one with the most distant star and the least little blade of grass. You shine as dew on the petal of the rose; you swing from star to star; you are part and parcel of all this manifestation."*

> *"Of course all are equal before the Lord; no-one has any special claim for preference, except probably the miserable and distraught."*

> *"You call yourself a sinner, a worm born in sin, wallowing in sin, essentially wicked. But, let someone who takes you at your word call you "Hello sinner!" you resent it. Why? Because your real nature is purity, peace, joy."*

> *"Remember your real nature is the same as the other man's; he is yourself known by another name. When you do a good deed, you are doing it to yourself; when you do a bad turn to someone, remember, you are injuring yourself; so avoid doing evil to others."*

> *"See yourself in all; love all as yourself. A dog caught in a*

room whose walls are mirrors sees in all the myriad reflections, not itself but rivals, competitors, other dogs which must be barked at. So it tires itself out by jumping on this reflection and that, and when the images also jump, it becomes mad with fury. The wise man, however, sees himself everywhere and is at peace; he is happy that there are so many reflections of himself all around him. That is the attitude which you must learn to possess, that will save you from needless bother."

2. *We live in ignorance of our true Nature and purpose of our existence.*

At different times Sathya Sai Baba has said that Man is the only being in the Universe which can change its nature from animal to Divine. We share in common with all creation a spark of Divinity called the Atman. The Atman is of the same essence as God. It is the mission of Man to develop the Divine qualities and reduce the animal or demonic qualities which we also possess.

"I condemn all signs of weakness and call the sense of weakness itself as a sin, an unpardonable sin. It is an insult to the heritage of Immortality which mankind deserves and must earn. Weakness, vacillation, despair; all these bring dishonor on Him who conferred on you the honour of 'Children of Immortality'. You are of the Nature of Strength. Do not bend and cringe and barter your self-respect. Do not believe that you are this little lump of body. You are the indestructible, immortal Soul (Atma) of the same nature as God Himself."

Sathya Sai Baba says that those who deny the existence of God are advertising their own limitations and ignorance. God is as close to us as we are to Him. When we feel distant from God, it is our doing, not His.

"You complain that God is invisible; but the fault is yours, not to recognize God in all His various manifestations. You are yourself a manifestation of God, but you do not know it."

In virtually every discourse, Sathya Sai Baba repeats the theme that the purpose of life is to find God in ourselves and the Universe.

"Man is endowed with many skills; he is offered many lives; he is shown many paths. The purpose of all these gifts is to develop in him the spirit of devotion and dedication and release him from the dual bubbles of joy and grief. When man visualizes the Universe as God, its capacity to confer the dual experience disappears; he knows the Truth and is calm. God is One and One only; "Ekam eve Adhivitiyam Brahma" (One only, without a second-Brahman, which is the immanent principle). So one must endeavour to know God, who is Truth."

3. *Our spirit has evolved from mineral existence to vegetable, animal and now as human.*

Many of the teachings of Baba are breath-taking in their clarity, simplicity and yet profound. In His "Dhyana Vahini" (p. 23-4), Baba describes the greatest Adventure that the universe has witnessed as follows:

"... Consider the condition of this world hundreds of thousands of years ago. At that time the globe was the scene of two things only. On one side was the fiery lava which shot forth from the volcanoes and the crevices that scarred the surface of the earth. The flood of destruction descended on all sides and spread fear and death in the regions around, as if the end of everything had come. On another side, the scarcely noticed molecules of living matter, the microscopic amoeba floated on the water or clung to the crevices among the rocks, keeping the spark of life safe and well protected.

Of these two, one boisterous and bright, the other, quiet and secluded, upon which would you have built your trust? At that time could anyone have believed that the future was with the amoeba or the animalcule? Who would have foreseen that these minute specks of life could hold out against the gigantic onslaught of molten lava and the earth-shaking upheaval?

That speck of Chaitanya or Consciousness won through nevertheless! Undaunted by fire and dust, by swooping gale or swallowing floods.

The amoeba, in process of time, by the sheer force of the Life-Principle it embodied, blossomed into goodness and strength of character, into art and music, into song and dance, scholarship and sadhana and martyrdom, into sainthood and even Avatars of Godhead!"

In a separate statement, rather reminiscent of the creation stories in Genesis, or the opening verses of John's Gospel, Baba declares:

"There was no one to know Who I am, till I created the World, at my pleasure, with one Word! Immediately, mountains rose up., rivers started flowing earth and sky were formed, oceans, seas, lands, and water-sheds, sun, moon and desert sands sprang out of nowhere, to prove my existence. Came all forms of beings, men, beasts, and birds, flying, speaking, hearing. All powers were bestowed upon them, under My orders. The first place was granted to Mankind, and my knowledge was placed in Man's mind."

4. The purpose of our existence is to realize our Divinity.

The notion that the true nature of Man is Divine may surprise many Christians. Yet Christians have been prepared to accept the idea that Man was created in the image of God and that God in the form of the Holy Spirit dwells within us. Over the centuries, a somewhat self-flagellating attitude has led to the idea that we are "poor miserable sinners", a concept which is admittedly difficult to reconcile with a being who is inherently Divine! Sathya Sai Baba calls upon us to drop the idea of our limitations and to look upon our strengths. We are all born as Children of God. As Jesus, as Son of God, became one with the Father, so do we all have the potential to cast off the limitations of human existence and become at one with God.

During several of His discourses, Baba has made statements such as:

"Man was born a mineral and died a mineral; then he promoted himself as a tree. He was long born a tree and died as a tree; in the process he got promoted as an animal; he has now risen into the status of man.... Now, alas! He is born as man and he dies as man. It is a greater shame if he slides into the beast or a beastly ogre. Praise is his due, only if he rises to the Divine status. That is the real fulfilment of his destiny".

Sathya Sai Baba emphasizes many times that the gap between humanity and Divinity is not unbridgeable, nor is it unreasonable to aspire to bridge the gap. Indeed, it is the purpose of our human existence that we should become one with the Divine. We all have the potential to realise and manifest our latent Divinity. God incarnates for the express purpose of helping humanity to take that step.

The idea is abroad in the West that only a few particularly pious souls need take the message of Jesus seriously enough to base their lives upon His teachings and that the message is true only for an ideal world, but not applicable to a world of "practical reality". Sathya Sai Baba affirms the essential content of what Jesus taught us and also affirms that far from being an optional extra in life, the fostering of spirituality is the whole purpose of our existence. He says:

"Man's life is meaningful only because he can use it to see God. The goal of life is the final merging into the sea, God. You should not fill life with the world; that will make it a vanity fair, an insanity fair. Listen to all such things as will draw you towards the Godhead; then think it over in the silence; make it part of your consciousness. This process of contemplation makes you a man."

"What is realisation? The moment you see your own beauty and are so filled with it that you forget all else, you are free of all bonds. Know that you are all the beauty, all the glory, all the power, all the magnitude of the Universe."

"Live in the consuming conviction that you are the Atman (Divine soul). This is the hard core of the teaching. The Atma it is that hears through the eyes, hears through the ears, handles through the fingers, moves through the feet. That is the basic 'you'."

5. It is through sin (impurities in our character) that we are separated from God.

Sathya Sai Baba stresses that following the path of righteousness is fundamental for our personal happiness as well as for the good of society. Humanity needs to transcend the animal aspects of our being in order to realise our Divine potential. Seeking short-term advantage from following the desires of the flesh, or behaving in ways which hurt other people, only work to our long-term detriment. Baba says:

"If the mind obeys the dictates of Discrimination then the individual gains. But if the mind becomes the slave of the senses, then woe be to the individual."

"Falsehood looks easy and profitable, but it binds you and pushes you into perdition."

"Contentment is the most precious wealth; greed brings misery in its train. Contentment alone can lead man to the goal of life, viz., the attainment of Divinity. Man has to acquire mastery over the foul urges in his own mind -- lust, anger, hatred, jealousy. Then only can he enjoy the Divine Peace that is his birthright. Every living being is on a pilgrimage, whether it is aware of it or not."

"All this misery is caused by mankind itself, not by any extraneous agency. Having all the instruments of joy and contentment in one's possession, if man is miserable it is due only to his perverseness, his stupidity. He has been warned over centuries by the Scriptures of all languages that he should give up greed and lust, give up the habit of catering to the senses,

give up the belief that he is just this body and nothing more. But yet he does not know the illness that is torturing him. The disease is called 'vitamin deficiency', as they say; the vitamins are Truth, Righteousness, Peace and Love. Take them and you recover; assimilate them into your character and conduct and you shine with fine mental and physical health."

6. Until we remove the impurities, we are condemned to repeated birth on Earth.

Where orthodox Christianity says that individuals take earthly body only once, Sathya Sai Baba is quite clear in affirming that we are born many times in human form and will continue to do so until we fulfil our inevitable destiny of merging with God.

As the doctrine of reincarnation will be a major stumbling block to many Christians, it is provided with fuller coverage in Chapter 10.

"You are all under sentence of imprisonment and are in this jail. There is no use hoping for reward when you work in jail; you have to work when you are ordered to, and work well, too. You cannot argue that rewards are not distributed justly and you are not entitled to desist from your allotted task. If you do so, your sentence may be extended or you will be transferred to another jail. On the other hand, if you quietly accept the sentence and go about your work without clamouring or mur-muring, your term is reduced and you are sent out with a cer-tificate that ensures a happy life, un-pestered by constables."

"Man is both an animal and divine being. He has risen from the animal level and is on the way to reveal his divinity. He should be vigilant that he does not slide into animal again. Man alone can rise in Godhood, for he is equipped with the endowment needed for the achievement."

"Some of you may imagine that it is a source of joy for the Lord to take human form. If you are in this state, you will not

feel so. I am always aware of the future, the past, as well as the present of each one of you. So I am not moved so much by mercy. Not that I am hard-hearted, or that I have no mercy or compassion. If you bolt the door fast, how can the rays of My grace be available to you? 'Swami', you cry, 'I have no eyes, I am yearning to see You, won't your heart melt at my plight?' Of course, his pitiable condition melts your hearts, it will not melt Mine. Since I know the past and the background, my re-action is different. If you only knew, your reaction, too, will be different. It is the consequence of evil, deliberately done in previous birth. So I have to allow the suffering to continue, modified only by some little compensation. I do not cause ei-ther joy or grief; you are the designer of both the chains that bind you."

7. By turning our lives over to God, He will purify our lives help us to manifest the Divine qualities which our ours by right.

Whereas it is the common view in the West that religion is something which is an optional extra for the pious few, Baba states that religion expresses the entire purpose of human existence. Without religion our lives are meaningless and useless.

Jesus, too, said:

"'You shall love the Lord your God with all your heart, and with all your soul, and with all your mind'. This is the greatest and first commandment." (Matthew 22 : 37-38)

The need for such a totality of commitment is reinforced by Baba in most of His discourses. Sometimes Baba scoffs at part-time devotees who still expect full-time protection from the Lord. Baba asks that we turn our lives over to God, in whatever Form we understand Him (or Her), and under whatever Name. Baba says that all Names are His, all Forms are His, and all prayers addressed to any Name of Form reach Him.

He does not expect the follower of any faith to abandon their own faith and turn to Himself. In fact, He has told Christians that they are to remain in their faith and live Christ's teachings in their lives. The need is to revitalise the churches, temples and synagogues, not to attract people away to different structures.

Some of His statements on these points are:

"Devotion is not a leisure-time job. Erase sensual desire; clear the mind of all blemish; then the Lord will be reflected therein as a mirror."

"The ego has to be fully curbed; the faith that not even a blade of grass can shiver in the wind without His being aware of it, and thus having caused it, has to be implanted in the mind."

"I am the Truth of Truth, I guide towards Truth, I manifest Truth, and when men realise Truth, they realise Me."

"I am the Embodiment of Love; Love is My Instrument. There is no creature without Love. The lowest loves itself at least, and its Self is God. So there are no atheists, though some might dislike Him or refuse Him as malarial patients dislike sweets or diabetic patients refuse to have anything to do with sweets! Those who preen themselves as atheists will one day, when their illness is gone, relish God and revere Him."

8. When Divinity becomes manifest in us, we are saved from the need for further birth in human form.

Sathya Sai Baba tells us in every discourse that the spirit which animates us is Divine. The divinity is overlaid with a great deal of ignorance and egoism so that it becomes invisible to us. When we purify ourselves by removing these bad qualities, Divinity manifests so that we become even as Jesus. This teaching causes some difficulty to some Christians who believe that when we are told that we are all God that the ultimate blasphemy is being committed. The truth is that Sathya Sai Baba is addressing such a statement to the Soul, which He calls the Atma. There is no way in which our anger, jealousies, desires, and petty mind are Divine.

Jesus implied that He lives in the heart of all people, when He said:

> *"'Come, you that are blessed by my Father, inherit the kingdom prepared for you from the foundation of the world; for I was hungry and you gave me food, I was thirsty and you gave me something to drink. . . . . '. Then the righteous will answer Him, 'Lord, when was it that we saw you hungry and gave you food, or thirsty and gave you something to drink? . . . . '. And the king will answer them, 'truly I tell you, just as you did it to the least of these who are members of my family, you did it to Me.'" – (Matthew 25 : 34-40 (abridged))*

Such a statement makes no sense unless it is accepted that God lives in the hearts of all people, even if not visible or detectable by our human consciousness. Sathya Sai Baba often states that *"Service to man is service to God"*. If by serving other people we are serving the God within them, it also follows that it is the God within us who is exercising the Divine service. When we live by the spiritual values of Truth, Love, Goodness and Serenity, in absolute form, we are manifesting Divine qualities. Baba says:

> *"Unless you have Love, you cannot claim kinship with the votaries of God; Love is the bridge which helps passage from birth to deathlessness, from death to birthlessness. When you rise from the Jiva-sense to the Deva-sense, (human-ness to God-ness) then there is no more birth or death. Liberation happens when you Love every being so intensely that you are aware of only ONE. Soak your heart in Love, soak your acts in righteousness, soak your emotions in compassion; then you attain God soonest."*

9. The Unity of God and Religion.

Sathya Sai Baba has said repeatedly that He has not come to establish a new religion. His mission is to restore the power of the existing religions. He castigates those who build new temples to Him and neglect the old ones. He says:

> *"All religions teach one basic discipline; the removal from the mind of the blemish of egoism of running after little joys. Every religion teaches man to fill his being with the Glory of God and evict the pettiness of conceit. It trains him in the methods of detachment and discrimination so that he may aim high and attain liberation.*

> *"Believe that all hearts are motivated by the One and Only God, that all Names in all languages and all forms man can conceive, denote the One and Only God. His adoration is best done by means of Love.*

> *"Cultivate that attitude of Oneness between men of all creeds, all countries and all continents. That is the message of Love I bring. That is the message I wish you to take to heart."*

> *"Along the lines already familiar to you, continue the worship of the God of your choice; then you will find that you are coming nearer and nearer to Me; for all Names are Mine and all Forms are Mine. There is no need to change after you have seen Me and heard Me."*

Post Script

Since writing this chapter in 1994 I have become conversant with quantum physics and how all matter and all beings are connected energetically. It is literately true, as Jesus said that whatever we do to other people (whether positive or negative) we do also to Him. It follows logically that as Christ lives in all people that what we do to Christ is also done to everyone. And what we do to others we do also to ourselves, even if the results are delayed. As I see it, this effect explains the law of Karma, an idea now endemic to Eastern philosophy but gaining ground in the West.

It is true that I cannot steal from another person without also stealing from myself, and whoever steals from me also steals from himself.

It also explains Jesus saying *"Love your enemies and pray for those who persecute you"* (Matthew 5:44). He says this because what we pray for others also comes back to us. As a practicing psychologist I often came across people who have been victims of crime, including assaults and rape. Many are caught up in anger and hatred for many years. It needs to be explained that as long as they harbor anger and hatred they are still bound to the offender both spiritually and psychologically. When they come to realize that the only person being affected by their anger is themselves and others who come into contact with them. It is not a matter of being "holy" or "saintly", it is a matter of mental and spiritual health.

I recommend Dean Radin's books. *The Conscious Universe*, and *Entangled Minds* for a scientific explanation on these points. (see Bibliography at end of book)

> "Let the different faiths exist, let them flourish, let the Glory of God be sung in all the languages and in a variety of tunes; that should be the ideal. Respect the differences between the faiths and recognise them as valid as far as they do not extinguish the flame of unity."
>
> Sathya Sai Baba

CHAPTER SEVEN

THE FIVE HUMAN VALUES

Jesus was compassion come in human form. He spread the spirit of compassion and conferred solace on the distressed and the suffering. good works always provoke the wicked, but one should not falter or fear when opposition obstructs. Jesus was the target for many mighty obstacles and He braved them all. As a result, His Name, story and message are still shedding splendorous light all over the world

Sathya Sai Baba

The most fundamental aspect of the mission of Sathya Sai Baba is the restoration of the primary human values. There are four primary values, viz *Sathya* (Truth), *Prema* (Pure Love), *Dharma* (Righteousness), and *Shanti* (Inner Peace). Commonly a fifth value is added called *Ahimsa* (Non-violence), which is a by-product of the others.

These values are absolute and are Divine by nature. They are necessary for the happiness of the individual and the functioning of mankind. Without these values, humanity degenerates into barbarism. With these values practised faithfully, humanity ascends to Divinity.

Sathya Sai Baba returns often to the theme that spiritual practice has direct benefits in mental and physical functioning:

> *"Devotion and morality are as important for the physical as they are for mental health. They free the mind from agitation, they feed it with joy and contentment; they quieten the nerves and even help bodily processes"*

Baba teaches that our character is the only real wealth we have. He points out that people who are remembered as great are so remembered, not through the material treasures they have won, or the power they wielded, but the character they displayed. Therefore the cultivation of good character is fundamental to worldly reputation as well as spiritual influence.

> *"It becomes essential to cleanse the mind through regular Sadhana, (spiritual practice) to tune the little will to the infinite will of God, so that it becomes merged in His Glory. Scholarship or skill, however deep and varied, have no cleansing power. They only add the alloys of pride and competition. Learned men are not necessarily good, nor are men with spiritual powers over nature above pride, envy and greed. Sathya, Dharma, Shanti and Prema are the hall-marks of a purified heart, where God is enshrined and is manifest."*

> *"Virtue is the life-breath; character is the backbone. Without that, no meritorious act will fructify. A characterless man is like a pot with many holes, useless for carrying water or storing it. Renounce and win peace; have and win troubles."*

The spiritual values are inter-dependent, in that as one becomes more loving, so one will also become more truthful, virtuous, peaceful and non-violent. However, each also has its own aspect, which are discussed below.

1. Sathya (Truth)

Sathya is, of course, the first name of Sathya Sai Baba. He has said *"Love is My Form, Truth is My Breath, Bliss is My Food."* Baba stresses the importance of Truthfulness as an absolute value. While He advises against speaking the truth when it will cause harm, Baba does not condone telling even a white lie. It is better to remain silent than to tell a truth which will hurt or a lie which will corrupt. When one is accustomed to telling small lies, then big lies become much easier and more likely. The effect of this is corruption of character.

"This teaching that Sathya (Truth) is the basis of Dharma which lays down individual and social duties and obligations and that Sathya is also the root of Prema and Shanti - this is the unique feature of Bharath (Indian) philosophy. Sathya is enough, no other God needs to be worshipped."

"Some people raise the question, 'How can we make a living if we adhere to Truth?' Well, you cannot escape death, whatever way you spend your days. It is far better to die, adhering to Truth, than to die sliding into falsehood. Falsehood looks easy and profitable; but it binds you and pushes you into perdition."

"It is much easier to speak the Truth and be done with it. What you have seen or heard or done, speak about these just as you saw or heard or did! And what is Dharma? Practising what you preach, doing as you practice in life. Earn virtuously; earn piously; live in the fear of God; live for reaching God. That is Dharma."

2. Prema (Pure Love)

Those who have made contact with Sathya Sai Baba know that His nature is love. He says that every action He takes is based on love for the world and His devotees. Even on the odd occasion when He shows anger, He says that this is done for the good of the person concerned, out of Love.

He advises His devotees:

> *"Give joy to all. Prema or Love is the means to achieve this ideal. When Love can bring even God nearer to you, how can it fail, where man is involved? That is the reason why Sai has declared: 'Start the day with Love; spend the day with Love, fill the day with Love; end the day with Love. That is the way to God.'"*

> *"If you love God, you have to love Man also."*

> *"Become fit for the vision of God, cultivating Prema in your heart, full of fragrance and uncontaminated by the pests of greed and egoism."*

> *"It is enough if Prema is cultivated, the Prema that knows no distinction between oneself and another, because all are but limbs of One corpus of God Almighty. Through Love alone, can the Embodiment of Love be gained. Here, no scholarship is needed; in fact, scholarship will be an impediment, for it caters to egoism and it breeds doubts and the desire for disputation and laurel of victory over others preening themselves as learned."*

The point is made often that the nature of God is Love, and that pure love *(Prema)* is Divine. When we love others, we love the God within them and therefore love God at the same time. When we hate or despise others, we are also hating and despising God. For that reason we are asked to love all:

> *"Rely on the Lord and accept whatever is your lot. He is in you, with you. He knows best what to give and when. He is full of Prema. That is My uniqueness: Prema. Prema is the special gift I bring, the special medium through which My Grace*

operates. That is the basis of all My acts. God is said to reside in everything. Yes. He resides as Prema. Devoid of Prema, the World becomes a cauldron of misery."

Baba says that it was through Love that God created all Creation. Love is the basic energy of the Universe and therefore the most powerful of all energies. Lack of Love causes illness in people and is behind most, if not all, problems. At the same time, Love which is limited is behind most evils. Love of one's country, a positive virtue, turns to evil when it is used to persecute or make war on peoples of other countries. Love which is pure, and can therefore be called Prema, is unconditional and showered on all.

"The spark of Love in you has to be cherished and fed, so that it may reach God; then, every being will be God; every act will be Divine; every reaction you get from the outside world will be charged with Prema and sweetened with nectar. You love the God in all beings and the God in all beings responds with Love. Love God, though tribulation may be your lot. Love Him, though you are refused and rebuked; for, it is only in the crucible of travail that the metal is purified and cleared of blemish. Adoration of God has to be through one name and one form; but, that should not limit your loyalty to that particular province only.

"Prema when you cultivate it, will remove the weeds of anger and of malice. It will blossom into peace and calm. My teaching is Prema, My message is Prema; My activity is Prema; and My way of living is Prema. There is nothing more precious than Love within human grasp.

3. Dharma (Righteousness)

"Dharma" is a word for which English has no exact equivalent. It is often translated variously as "righteousness", "right conduct", "code of conduct", "duty", "justice", and "obligation." Derived from the root

"dha" meaning "wear", *Dharma* is that which is worn. As clothes maintain the dignity of the person who wears them, so *Dharma* is the measure of the dignity of a people.

Baba makes the point that *Dharma* is behind all relationships between people, their path in the world, their conduct in business or within the family. When *Dharma* is strong, then relationships within society are correct and just. When *Dharma* declines, then evil abounds and chaos takes over.

In these days, *Dharma* is declining rapidly and humanity is sinking into misery, chaos, crime, fear and mutual hatred. Baba makes the point many times that the home is where *Dharma* should be fostered and developed. When respect for each other within the home declines and the values of morality and religion are not taught, then the decay of dharma must affect the fabric of society and the nation.

Sathya Sai Baba has said:

> *"Birds, beasts and trees have not deviated from their nature; they are still holding it valid. Man alone has disfigured it, in his crude attempt to improve upon it. So, the Avatar has to come as Man among men, and move as friend, well-wisher, kinsman, guide, teacher, healer and participant among men. He has come to restore Dharma and when man follows Dharma, He is pleased and content."*

> *"Man is born for the attainment of joy, not for sheer eating and revelling. Real and lasting Joy can be won only by a life led along the path of Dharma which makes the inherent Divinity of Man shine forth; Illumination is the purpose of life and of the recurring sequence of birth and death. Man has in him the spark of Divinity, which is Omnipresent, Omniscient, Omnipotent, and immanent in the entire Universe. In order to become ever aware of this innate Reality, man must learn the technique laid down by the Scriptures, revealed by the same Divinity."*

"Dharma purifies the mind and leads you to God. It creates a taste for the Name and Form of God. When you love the Name and Form of God, you will naturally respect and obey the command of God, His Word which is found in the Scriptures. Have the Name on the tongue and Form in the eye; and the demon, called Aasa, unending desire, will fly from your mind, leaving joy and content therein. This kind of constant dwelling on the indwelling God will promote Love for all beings. You will then see good in others and you will strive to do good to others."

"Dharma is the road for individual and social progress in this World and, through this World, to the next. It is eternal, basic and fundamental. The principles may not be altered or adjusted to suit personal whims or pressing problems that appear formidable to the eyes of some individuals or group of persons. It is like the mother who has to be accepted, not like the wife whom you can choose or discard."

"Dharma is the root of this World. Obey it and you are happy. The evil man is a coward, haunted by fear. He has no peace within him. Respect for the parents who started you in life and brought you into this World, together with the vast and varied treasure of experience, is the first lesson that Dharma teaches. Gratitude is the spring which feeds that respect. It is a quality that is fast disappearing in the World today. Respect for the teacher, for the elders and for the wise is on the decline. That is why Dharma is fast disappearing and losing its hold."

"If one loses wealth, he may regain it by some means or other. If he loses health, some doctor might prescribe a tonic to win it back. If one loses status and authority he may, by sheer luck, gain them back. If Virtue is lost, it is lost forever; nothing can restore the pristine purity. So one has to be ever vigilant and should never slacken."

4. Shanti (Peace)

Shanti is a spiritual value inextricably woven into the fabric with the others. The word is sometimes translated as "tranquillity", "serenity" or "equanimity". It is the peace known in *"the still small voice of God"*. Peace of mind, heart and soul is sought after by all people, but so seldom found. It is easily disturbed when one chases after worldly pleasures. When ego and desire become rampant in the human heart, *Shanti* disappears. Baba says

> *"Ambition to earn fame in the world, to gain some position of authority over fellow-men, to lead luxurious life - this can never ensure Shanti, Mental Peace. Mental Peace is the result of quite different attainments. Wealth cannot command it, nor authority commandeer it!"*

> *"Shanti has detachment as the basic quality. The sea which likes to gather and possess lies low; the cloud that likes to renounce and give is high up in the sky."*

> *"Shanti endows man with an unruffled mind and steady vision. The Prayer for Shanti is usually repeated thrice: 'Om Shanti, Shanti, Shanti', since peace is prayed for, in the physical, mental and spiritual planes."*

> *"Faith has to be cultivated, first and foremost. It has to be nurtured in Love. Love is fostered by Shanti. Shanti can be got only when there is full reliance on God and complete surrender to the Divine Will."*

> *"Joy is your birth-right, Shanti is your inmost nature. The Lord is your Staff and Support. Do not discard it; do not be led away from the path of faith by stories invented by malice and circulated by spite. Take up the Name of God, any of the innumerable ones, any that appeals to you most and the Form appropriate to that Name and start repeating it. From now on, that is the Royal Road to ensure Joy and Peace, that will train you in the feeling of brotherhood and remove enmity towards fellowmen.*

5. Ahimsa (Non-violence)

The value of non-violence incorporates all the others. Sathya Sai Baba says that,

> *"When Love illumines thought, Truth is revealed. When Love motivates action, it is transformed into Right Conduct. When Love saturates feelings, it becomes calm and serene and ensures Peace. When anger, envy, greed and hatred are cast away, Love dawns as understanding and Non-violence reigns supreme. This is the reason why man is told, 'Love thy neighbour as thyself', for the neighbour is no other than Myself."*

Ahimsa shows itself as total respect for other people and all creation. There is a clear relationship between Ahimsa and the other virtues as is shown in the readings which follow. Violence is not only physical in its manifestation, but is also an internal state in the form of anger. Therefore refraining from violence also entails refraining from violence in mood and thought as well as deed. When the principle of Ahimsa is fully understood, the desire to eat meat drops away. Swami advises His devotees to eat only vegetarian food, and will not permit non-vegetarian foods into the Ashram.

> *"Ahimsa (Non-violence) means avoiding causing harm to anyone by thought, word or deed. Out of selfishness and self-interest, men do not practise this estimable virtue. All evils arise from the sense of 'I' and 'Mine'. This trait can be eliminated only by developing purity in thought, word and deed. "*

Ahimsa is expressed in the best-known spiritual statement which is known as "The Golden Rule", found in various forms in almost all cultures. Swami says:

> *"Every man should so lead his life that no pain is caused by him to any living thing. That is his supreme duty. Also, it is the prime duty of everyone who has had the chance of this human*

> *birth, to spare part of his energies occasionally for prayer, meditation, or repetition of the Lord's name, and his life in Truth, Rightfulness, Peacefulness and good works which are of service to others. One must be as afraid of doing acts that are harmful to others or deeds that are sinful, as one is afraid to touch fire or disturb a cobra. One must have as much attachment and steadfastness in carrying out good works that make others happy and in worshipping the Lord, as one now has in accumulating riches. This is the true Dharma of man. It is to strengthen this type of goodness that the Lord incarnates Himself in human form."*

Swami teaches that the values He teaches pervade every aspect of human activity. As the following quote demonstrates, Ahimsa lies behind respect for the Earth and its resources, as well as respecting the environment of other people.

> *"In the business world and in the context of industrial management, Ahimsa has a wider social meaning than merely avoiding harm to others. The avoidance of pollution of the atmosphere or of natural resources like rivers, is one of the ways in which an enterprise can practise non-violence. In such ways, a great deal of good can be done by business managers who adhere to the basic human values and who adopt a spiritual approach to the tasks of the business world."*

Sathya Sai Baba speaks against the glorification of violence in cinemas and television and says watching of such "entertainment" is disruptive of spiritual growth, particularly in young people.

"Jesus was a Messenger of God; 'but note this also; all of you are messengers of God You are all His children. Jesus and His Father are One. You and God are also one, and you can become aware of it. Whatever activity you may be engaged in, wherever you may be, however you may fare, be convinced that you are ever in God, that all is Divine, that all acts are offerings to the glory of God, and thus make your lives full and fruitful."

Sathya Sai Baba

CHAPTER EIGHT

SOME OTHER IMPORTANT TEACHINGS

Sathya Sai Baba is familiar with the teachings and sacred books of all religions in the world, though He is known never to have studied any of them in a formal sense. He often gives guidance and instruction to His students and devotees which adds new light on old teachings, as well as reconciling the diverse accounts in different religions.

Baba is also keen to reconcile the teachings of science and spirituality. In the Universities which He has founded in every state of India, all teaching has a spiritual basis and orientation. For example, courses in management also teach the need for Truth and Righteousness as values on which businesses are run and managed. Respect for Creation in the form of the Earth and its resources are taught as well as human values. The Gospel of the Golden Age integrates all human knowledge into a unified approach to all human affairs. There is no field of human conduct or endeavour which is not touched upon in the teaching of Sathya Sai Baba. Spirituality embraces all aspects of life.

Control of the Senses

The senses have value for the physical aspect of our being in dealing with life on Earth. They relate to the animal aspect of us and become a hindrance to spirituality if our lives become enmeshed in sensual gratification. Therefore control of the senses is recommended in all religions. In Christianity it has been fundamental in the monastic tradition and in those called to celibacy.

At least some discipline of the senses is necessary for any spiritual path. Sathya Sai Baba stresses the need for the senses to be under our control, rather than allowing the senses to control us. His teachings in these matters are not new, but they remind us of the priorities of our existence and the need for moderation in the use of the senses.

In addition to traditional teachings on sense control, Sathya Sai Baba stresses the need for control of the tongue. Some of Baba's teachings on this matter are:

> *"The tongue is the armour of the heart; it guards one's life. Loud talk, long talk, wild talk, talk full of anger and hate, all these affect the health of man. They breed anger and hate in others; they wound, they excite, they enrage, they estrange.*

> *"Why is silence said to be golden? The silent man has no enemies, though he may not have friends. He has the leisure and the chance to dive within himself and examine his own faults and failings. He has no more inclination to seek them in others.*

> *"If your foot slips, you earn a fracture; if your tongue slips, you fracture some one's faith or joy. That fracture can never be set right; that wound will fester for ever. Therefore use the tongue with great care. The softer you talk, the less you talk, the sweeter you talk, the better for you and the world"*

Ceiling on Desires

Sathya Sai Baba prescribes certain disciplines both for the good of the devotees, the sake of society and the Earth itself. The ceiling on desires programme enjoins people to limit their use and wastage of four resources. These resources are:

Time, Money, Energy, Food

Ceiling on Desires for Time

Sathya Sai Baba frequently reminds his followers that time is life and that waste of time is waste of life. Human life offers a unique chance. It is short enough as it is, without wasting it on frivolous, time-wasting pursuits. The purpose of life is to realise one's divinity, and anything short of that goal is to waste the chance which human birth affords.

Frequently, He urges us to be aware that our time is limited, and that we have no idea when it is going to be cut short. He also tells us that living in this age is itself a considerable blessing and there is so much more opportunity for spiritual growth in a world which opposes spiritual values. Baba often tells His devotees to avoid cinemas, television, novels and other recreational activities which are destructive in nature.

Ceiling on Desires for Money

There is injustice in having insufficient money, and injustice in hoarding more than is needed. The lust for acquiring excessive wealth is behind war and crime. When people start hoarding money, they are never satisfied with the amount which they have accumulated, no matter how great it is. In present days the inequality in distribution of the wealth of the world is obscene. Swami says:

> *"The richest man on earth is the one with least desires, and the poorest man on earth is the one with most desires"*

Ceiling on Desires for Energy

The principle of conservation of energy is tied both to internal physical energy as well as to energy resources such as fuel and electricity.

With this principle at work, much of the plunder of the Earth for oil, firewood and other energy sources would be substantially reduced, as would inequality between peoples and pollution of the environment.

Sathya Sai Baba has indicated that in the Golden Age there will be a balance restored between the energy which is used and the ability of the Earth to sustain the level of use. His message reinforces the efforts of environmentalists concerned for the future of the planet.

Ceiling on Desires for Food

Over consumption of food is a cause of many health problems, as is the quality of food. Swami advises people not to indulge in food for sensuous reasons, or to indulge in gluttony. He tells us that the tongue can cause offence in two ways, by speaking evil, or by wanting particular taste sensations.

He has advised His followers to regard food as a medicine which we have to take because of the frailty of the body in requiring physical nourishment. In this spirit, we are advised to limit the quantity and nature of food ingested. As Swami says, we should eat to live, not live to eat.

Meditation on the Name of the Lord

Sathya Sai Baba teaches us that the surest way to God in this age is to keep the Name of God in the forefront of our consciousness. Other religions have prescribed various disciplines and meditations for this purpose. Christians have perhaps been less mindful of the need to keep God in mind than have followers of some other faiths. For Christians, keeping the Name of Jesus in mind constantly is appropriate.

In one of His Christmas discourses, Baba said:

> *"Jesus said 'I am the way . . . I am the door; if anyone enters by Me, he will be saved . . .' Choose a picture of Jesus that inspires your heart. Keep it before you above your prayer altar. Keep a picture of Jesus where you work. Carry one with you wherever you go. When you find yourself calling Jesus' name*

almost automatically from the moment you awaken until you lose consciousness at night, you are ready to start contemplating the Form of Jesus shown in your picture of Him.

"As you repeat the Name in the morning prayer period, begin to picture in the mind's eye the Form you love so well. Start with His hair. Draw each lock of hair separately. Then fill in His facial features one by one. You may do this with your eyes open or closed, but be sure not to stop calling His Divine Name while you are visualising His Form. Do this throughout the day whenever you have a few minutes.

"Always use the same picture. Don't use Jesus the shepherd in the morning, Jesus as a twelve year old in the temple at noon and the infant Jesus at night. Remain with whichever form you choose. Don't change it. Let it settle permanently in your heart.

"When your thoughts wander from the Form of Jesus, focus on the Name of Jesus. If the mind wanders from the Name, continue creating the Form. If the mind wanders a hundred times, bring it back a hundred times. As the Form stabilises, you will see Jesus more and more as the living being He really is. You will see Him and feel the warmth of His closeness and loving guidance, no matter what happens throughout the day."

"People ask, what is in a name? It is just an assortment of sounds. My words, too, are assortments of sound, but when they enter your hearts, you feel content, you feel encouraged, do you not? Words have tremendous power; they can arouse emotions and they can calm them. They direct, they infuriate, they reveal, they confuse; they are potent forces that bring up great reserves of strength and wisdom. Therefore have faith in the Name and repeat it whenever you get the chance."

"Christ announced Himself as the Messenger of God. He identified His body as having been given to Him for alleviating human misery and serving the helpless and the homeless. He denied the demands of the flesh and devoted His skills and strength to relieve agony and pain. Then, when the consciousness rose to the level of the mind, He became aware that He was the Son of God. He strove hard to discover the distinction between appearance and Reality, between Truth and mental image, and He became aware of the higher levels of consciousness which transcend the vagaries of the mind. From that peak of intelligence, He became aware that "I and my Father are one. And both are one single manifestation of the Divine Essence, the Holy Spirit."

Sathya Sai Baba

CHAPTER NINE

THE TEACHINGS OF JESUS AND SATHYA SAI BABA COMPARED

Sathya Sai Baba affirms and supports the teachings and message of Jesus. There are many parallels, of which the following are but a few examples:

Jesus

"Whoever wishes to be great among you must be your servant, and whoever wishes to be first among you must be your slave; just as the Son of Man came not to be served but to serve, and to give his life a ransom for many." Matthew 20 : 26-28

Baba

"Man can realise his mission on the earth only when he knows himself as Divine and when he reveres all others as Divine. And, man has to worship God in the form of Man. God appears before him as a blind beggar, an idiot, a leper, a child, a decrepit old man, a criminal or madman. You must see even behind those veils the Divine Embodiment of Love, Power, and Wisdom, the Sai and worship Him through Seva (service).

"Individuals are very anxious to acquire positions of authority. They are not considering the need for fulfilling any of their responsibilities. In the case of one who understands his duty and responsibility, it follows automatically that he will in due course get a position and authority. But one who does not understand his duty will never be able to acquire a position. In order to evolve oneself into a balanced individual service is an essential quality. This idea of service has the good quality of removing ego in man. It promotes love and affection. It takes him away from the aspect of worldly attachments and puts him on the path to the Divine. This idea of service also explains to him the meaning of divinity. It can give widespread pleasure and bliss for the entire mankind. In fact, service is the first step along the spiritual path.

"When we think of service, we seem to think of work which is a lowly kind of work, usually done by a servant. This kind of association of ideas, where service is thought of as something lowly, is not correct. In the context of service, we should realise that God himself does a lot of service in the world in many ways. We are familiar with the concept of an Avatar when God takes birth in human form to re-establish dharma or put back righteousness in its high place thus doing service to the world.

"Service is the worship you offer to God in the heart of everyone.

"Duty is God. Work is worship. Even the tiniest work is a flower placed at the feet of God.

Jesus

"If any want to become my followers, let them deny themselves and take up their cross and follow me. For those who want to save their life will lose it, and those who lose their life for my sake will find it. For what will it profit them if they gain the whole world

but forfeit their life? Or what will they give in return for their life? Matthew 16 : 24-26

Baba

"Service without idea of self is the very first step in the spiritual progress of man.

"If a man wants to lead a peaceful life, he must realise the importance of sacrifice. The truth in the statement that immortality can be obtained through sacrifice alone should be understood well.

"The very basis of spiritual progress is the denial of the I, and the joyful acceptance of the We, which is but the merging of the I in He.

"Attachments make you lose your freedom. You cannot move freely when you are encumbered with burdens. Less luggage, more comfort, is a slogan for the journey of life. Reduce desires, loosen attachments; you win freedom."

Jesus

"Truly I tell you, unless you change and become like children, you will never enter the kingdom of heaven. Whoever becomes humble like this child is the greatest in the kingdom of heaven. Whoever welcomes one such child in my name welcomes me." Matthew 18 : 2-5

Baba

"The babe is the inheritor of immortality; as it is unaffected by anxiety that haunts the adult.

"When the elders speak it is difficult to discover whether it is truth, scandal or untruth. But children are plain-spoken. They have not discovered that success in the worldly sense is dependent on cleverness in the short run; though in the long run it is honesty and

plain-speaking that bring maximum profit. That is why it is said that you must either become as simple and straight forward as a child or as wise and discriminating as a deeply learned scholar to win the Grace of God.

Jesus

"Then someone came to him and said, 'Teacher, what good deed must I do to have eternal life?' And he said to him, 'Why do you ask me about what is good? There is only one who is good. If you wish to enter into life, keep the Commandments. He said to him, 'Which ones?' And Jesus said, 'You shall not murder; You shall not commit adultery; You shall not steal; You shall not bear false witness; Honour your father and mother; also, You shall love your neighbour as yourself." The young man said to him, 'I have kept all these; what do I still lack?" Jesus said to him, 'If you wish to be perfect, go, sell your possessions, and give the money to the poor, and you will have treasure in heaven; then come, follow me." Matthew 19 : 16-21

Baba

"What exactly is your duty? Let Me summarise it for you. First, tend your parents with love and reverence and gratitude. Second, speak the truth and act virtuously. Third, whenever you have a few moments to spare, repeat the Name of the Lord, with the Form in mind. Fourth, never indulge in talking ill of others or trying to discover faults in others. And finally, do not cause pain to others, in any form.

"Keep away from the ten-fold sins, the three physical, the four verbal, and the three mental. Physical tendencies are: Injury to life, adulterous desire and theft. The verbal sins are: False alarm, cruel speech, jealous talk and lies. The mental attitudes are: Greed, envy and the denial of God.

"Try to prevent the five sins that the body commits: Killing, Adultery, Theft, Drinking intoxicants and the Eating of Flesh. It is a great help for the highest life if these are kept as far away as possible.

Jesus

"'You shall love the Lord your God with all your heart, and with all your soul and with all your mind. This is the greatest and first commandment.' And a second is like it: 'You shall love your neighbour as yourself.' On these two commandments hang all the law and the prophets." Matthew 22 : 37-40

Baba

"Love all beings, that is enough. Love with no expectation of return; love because your very nature is love. Love because that is the form of worship you know and like. When others are happy, be happy likewise. When others are in misery, try to alleviate their lot to the best of your ability. Practice Love through Seva (selfless service). By this means you will realise Unity and get rid of the ego that harms.

"The spark of love in you has to be cherished and fed so that it may reach God; then every being will be God and every act will be Divine. Every reaction you get from the outside world will be charged with prema (highest love) and sweetened with nectar. You love the God in all beings and the God in all beings responds with love. Love God, though tribulation may be your lot. Love Him, though you are refused and rebuked; for it is only in the crucible of travail that the metal is purified and cleared of blemish. Love alone can alleviate anxiety and allay fear.

"Devotion should not be confined to the four walls of your prayer room, or the few minutes you spend in contemplation. It is full time

spiritual practice. Your devotion has to be expressed as worship of everyone, as a living embodiment of Divinity. See God in everyone, even in persons whom you regard as your enemies. Practise that broad, inclusive type of love.

"More than all other forms of love, your first effort should be to fix your love on the Lord.

"Develop love, scatter love, reap love; there is no religion higher than that. That is the noblest seva."

Jesus

"Woe unto you, scribes and Pharisees, hypocrites! For you lock people out of the kingdom of heaven. For you do not go in yourselves, and when others are going in, you stop them." Matthew 23 : 13-14

Baba

"The worst Karma (action) is to do the opposite of what you preach: to deny by the hand that you dole out of your mouth. If you cannot act up to your declarations, keep quiet; do not go about advising and advertising that you are hypocrites. Do not preach Dharma (righteousness) while decrying it in deed. Dharma is steady, unchanging, it can never decline. What happens is: those who have to practise Dharma decline in faith and steadfastness. By practise is man judged; not by the precepts that he pours forth.

"The power of discrimination is definitely more valuable than bookish knowledge, wealth and physical strength. The co-ordination of thoughts, words and deeds is the first step in spiritual growth. Lack of correlation between ideas, utterances and actions leads to self-delusion, hypocrisy and spiritual bankruptcy."

Jesus

"You have heard that it was said, 'An eye for an eye and a tooth for a tooth.' But I say to you, Do not resist an evil-doer. But if anyone strikes you on the right cheek, turn the other also; and if anyone wants to sue you and take your coat, give your cloak as well; and if anyone forces you to go one mile, go also the second mile. Give to everyone who begs from you, and do not refuse anyone who wants to borrow from you. Matthew 5 : 38-42

Baba

"I command you: never hate others, or wish evil of them or talk ill of them. Then only can you gain peace.

"Even when you are slandered, you should not lose balance. Put up with slander and scandalising talk. Anger is the chief enemy of spiritual work."

Jesus

"You have heard that it was said, 'You shall love your neighbour and hate your enemy.' But I say to you, Love your enemies and pray for those who persecute you, so that you may be children of your Father in heaven: for he makes his sun rise on the evil and on the good, and sends rain on the righteous and on the unrighteous. For if you love those who love you, what reward do you have? Do not even the tax collectors do the same? And if you greet only your brothers and sisters, what more are you doing than others'? Do not even the Gentiles do the same? Be perfect, therefore. as your heavenly Father is perfect." Matthew 5 : 43-48

Baba

"When someone insults you or defames you or ignores you, accept it with a smile; this is the way of the world; it is basically ungrateful, ill-mannered. Say to yourself:

"They are doing me a good turn, my strength is under trial, I should not yield to anger or resentment."

"Tell yourself such invigorating things and be quiet, with a smile of triumph on your lips.

"There was once a monk (a Sanyasin) who was roundly abused by a gang of mischievous young men. He said, 'Carry on! Enjoy yourselves, I see you are happy at the chance. This is exactly what I wish for you.'

"When you do not accept the insult someone casts on you, it goes back to the person who indulged in it first; a registered letter that is not accepted returns to the sender. Do not damage your mental peace by receiving the letter and reading the contents. Refuse to receive it. You have a chance of correcting the wrong-doers too; accept it and you join the gang of mischief-makers, so be warned!

"The weapon of love disarms every opponent. Love begets love; it will be reflected back, it will have only love as a reaction. Shout 'Love', the echo from the other person's heart will also be 'Love'."

Jesus

"Beware of practicing your piety before others in order to be seen by them; for then you have no reward from your Father in heaven.

"So whenever you give alms, do not sound a trumpet before you, as the hypocrites do in the synagogues and in the streets, so that they may be praised by others. Truly I tell you, they have received their reward. But when you give alms, do not let your left hand know what your right hand is doing, so that your alms may be done in secret; and your Father who sees in secret will reward you."

"And whenever you pray, do not be like the hypocrites; for they love to stand and pray in the synagogues and at the street corners, so that

they may be seen by others. Truly I tell you, they have received their reward. "But whenever you pray, go into your room and shut the door and pray to your Father who is in secret; and your Father who sees in secret will reward you." Matthew 6 : 1-6

Baba

"Act, but do not hanker after the fruit. Do not complain that you did not get public recognition for money that you gave to some Trust. Fruits, whether good or bad, you have to consume; so the best means of liberating yourself from the consequences is to ignore the fruit and act for the sake of the action only.

"Do not parade your spiritual practices in the market place as some crazy people do now. Do not yearn for approbation and appreciation from the public. Pray that God may approve, accept and appreciate your twaddle and your prattle."

Sathya Sai Eternal Heritage Museum

In it, is depicted every aspect of man's eternal search for the inner meaning of life, and the many forms of religious worsip throughout the world

The Christian chapel in the Eternal Heritage Museum

CHAPTER TEN

REINCARNATION IN CHRISTIAN DOCTRINE

"You may say that progress is possible only through God's Grace; but though My Heart is soft as butter it melts only when there is some warmth in your prayer. Unless you make some disciplined effort, some spiritual striving (sadhana), Grace cannot descend on you. The yearning, the agony of the unfulfilled aim, that is the warmth that melts My Heart. That is the anguish that wins Grace."

Sathya Sai Baba

The idea of reincarnation may be seen as a stumbling block to some Christians who believe it is contrary to the teachings of Jesus. The fact is that until the Second Council of Constantinople in 553 AD, early Christians (including the great Origen) believed in reincarnation. It is notable that the Pope was absent from this Council (even though he was staying in Constantinople at the time), and the vote was not unanimous, being split in the proportion of 3 to 2.

An interesting account of the dropping of the doctrine is provided by Holger Kersten:

> *"The damning of the rebirth doctrine is traceable to a personal attack by the Emperor Justinian, which never entered the protocols of the Council. Justinian's ambitious wife, who actually held the reins of power . . . began her swift rise to power as a courtesan. In order to free herself of her shameful past, she later ordered the abuse and death of 500 of her former 'colleagues'. Because she would have to suffer the full consequences of these cruel deeds in a subsequent life according to the Karma doctrine, she set about having the whole magnificent teaching of rebirth simply abolished. . . .*

> *"Emperor Justinian then proceeded to declare war on the teachings of Origen as early as 543 A.D., without considering the views of the Pope, and had them damned by a special Synod. In his works De Principiis and Contra Celsum, the great Church Father, Origen (185-253 A.D.) had quite clearly acknowledged the prenatal existence of the soul and its dependence on earlier actions. He thought that only in the light of reincarnation could certain scriptural passages of the New Testament be explained."*

> *"The Council of Constantinople, the fifth of the Councils, was more or less a private meeting organised by Justinian, at which he (together with the vassals subject to him) imposed a ban and a curse on the pre-existence of the soul, despite the protest of Pope Virgilius, with the publication of his Anathemata."*

Kersten concludes:

> *"The prohibition of the rebirth doctrine is therefore simply an error of history and lacking all ecclesiastical validity"*

Such a conclusion will no doubt surprise and challenge most Christians, but it is an issue which Christianity must face up to. While it is clearly an error to accept doctrines which are false, it is an equal error to deny doctrines which are true. To persist in claiming that the soul for each of us takes birth once only, when there is a large body of evidence that this is not the case is as unreasonable as the Church's former insistence that the Earth was flat.

There is no evidence in the accepted Gospels that Jesus directly taught the idea of reincarnation, though He also is not recorded as denying it. The fact that there is no record on this matter should not invalidate it, as we have only small samples of His teachings, recorded many years after he spoke them, and these records have been partially censored by the early Church to suit the opinions of the ruling bodies of the time.

There is evidence within the Gospels that reincarnation was accepted in the time of Jesus, who seems to have referred to it as though it were part of the accepted ideas of His day. He was never recorded as repudiating it or teaching that it was false.

What did Jesus mean in Matthew 11 : 14, when, speaking of John the Baptist, He said: *"This is Elijah which is to come"?* Or again, in Mark 9 : 11

> *"Then they asked him, 'Why do the scribes say that Elijah must come first?' He said to them, 'Elijah is indeed coming first to restore all things. How then is it written about the Son of Man, that he is to go through many sufferings and be treated with contempt? But I tell you that Elijah has come, and they did to him whatever they pleased, as it is written about him.'"*

And from Matthew 17 : 10-13

> *"And the disciples asked him, 'Why, then, do the scribes say that Elijah must come first?' He replied. 'Elijah is indeed coming and will restore all things; but I tell you that Elijah has already come, and they did not recognize him, but they did to him whatever they pleased. So also the Son of Man is about to*

*suffer at their hands.' <u>Then the disciples understood that he
was speaking to them about John the Baptist.</u>"*

It would be hard to put into clearer language the idea that John the
Baptist was a reincarnation of Elijah. However, many Christians will
still use whatever convoluted logic they feel is necessary to deny whatever is written that does not conform to their prejudices.

In Matthew 16 : 13, we read that Jesus asked His disciples,

*"Now when Jesus came into the district of Caesarea
Philippi, he asked his disciples. 'Who do people say that the
Son of Man is?' And they said 'Some say John the Baptist,
but others Elijah, and still others Jeremiah or one of the
prophets."*

The idea of reincarnation was obviously common and Jesus did not
rebuke them for talking nonsense or condemn the idea.

Without such an understanding of reincarnation, some passages in the
Bible would not make sense.

*"With the <u>Spirit and power of Elijah</u> he will go before him, to
turn the hearts of parents to their children . . . ."* Luke 1 : 17

A Roman writer, Josephus wrote of reincarnation as being a common
Jewish belief in the time of Christ: *"They say that all souls are incor-
ruptible, but that the souls of good men are only removed into other
bodies".*

The Essenes, a prominent sect at the time of Jesus whose teachings were very similar to those of Jesus are known to have taught
reincarnation.

Present-day Evidence

Other arguments in favour of reincarnation come from experiences
of people who have been regressed, apparently into past lives, under
hypnosis or under stress.

Following from the work of Mesmer, who is credited with discovering hypnosis, some early psychoanalysts in the footsteps of Freud found that patients who regressed to early childhood memories could also go back to time in the womb and even earlier. In exploring this phenomena, the early practitioners attempted to find explanations other than reincarnation for the results of their work, but were forced to conclude that they were tapping into a real, if puzzling, effect.

Inevitably, certain practitioners explored past life regression in systematic ways and produced results which could be replicated by other practitioners. Thus the methods used could be called scientific, even if the orthodox scientific community (particularly in the Western world) have great trouble in accepting the validity of the conclusions from this work.

Some of the earliest materials in this area are found in "the Bloxham Tapes". Bloxham was a hypnotist who regressed several hundreds of people under hypnosis and had them recall past lives. The tapes were transcribed and a BBC investigator followed up on a number of the transcriptions to check for historical accuracy and probability of the memories being valid. Historians were asked to comment on details, many of which were confirmed through other sources. A number of details were not known to historians, but were consistent with what was known of the times, while other points suggested some interesting new hypotheses. Taken together, the Bloxham tapes present some highly convincing material in favour of a theory of reincarnation.

There is also an impressive amount of anecdotal material of people under stress who unexpectedly have apparent memories of similar events in previous lives. Other people, in visiting new places, have a feeling that they have been there before, and can produce clear descriptions of the places and the people who lived in them relating to earlier times.

There are now practitioners who specialize in recovering memories of previous lives in their clients. Even people who do not believe in reincarnation have produced such "memories".

Some researchers have found that children, of both East and West, report memories of a past life which often fade as they grow older. Parents rarely encourage children to carry on with strange talk about life in another time. Professor Ian Stevenson of was a Canadian-born U.S. psychiatrist. He worked for the University of Virginia School of Medicine for fifty years. He studied some 3,000 cases of apparent reincarnation, and provided evidence which should convince any honest enquirer.

Theological Implications

The doctrine of only one birth per soul raises some troublesome issues for Christianity.

Christians have generally asserted that those who hear the Gospel and reject it are condemned to Hell. This raises the question as to what happens to people born before Jesus who did not have the opportunity to hear the Gospel. The response of one school of thought is that in the last days, there shall be a general resurrection in physical form of all those who died without the chance to hear the Gospel and they shall have the opportunity then to accept Christ as Savior. Given the options which would be presented under these conditions, there would have to be a very high conversion rate, though those so converted may feel that they were hardly exercising free-will!

There are issues around what is supposed to happen to people born into other faiths who hear the Gospel but continue to practice their own faiths. The hard-line Christian will assert that they will go to Hell without question.

This line become increasingly unreasonable when questions are raised about people such as Mahatma Gandhi, who exemplified Christian virtues while remaining a Hindu. I have heard Christians assert that Gandhi would go to Hell, while the greatest rogue and sinner who accepts Christ will enter into the bosom of the Lord.

Such adherence to strict theology suggests that God is neither just, nor merciful, nor even sensible. This conclusion is patently false to anyone of any spiritual sensitivity. The promulgation of hard-line Christian teachings have created huge barriers between Christianity and other religions in the past, and will be a stumbling block in the future until Christians can view God as Jesus did. Conversely, the acceptance of reincarnation as a fact will do much to make God's plan for ourselves and Creation itself much more intelligible. It will also assist in turning people back to God.

People of other religions have often looked at Christians, the lives they lead, and the amount of love, truth, peace and purity in their lives, and have concluded that Christianity is not for them. Christians have often neglected to practice what Jesus told them to do and have been condemned as hypocrites by other people who understand essential spirituality.

Conclusions

The issue of reincarnation is a difficult one for Christians. It is a topic on which many books have been written, and those who still find the issue a hurdle should consult some of those available, of which some are listed in the Bibliography.

Christians would be well advised to keep an open mind on the issue until they have satisfied themselves either way. The historic church did not always oppose the doctrine of reincarnation, and many Christians even today feel comfortable in accepting a belief in reincarnation alongside a living faith in Jesus Christ as Lord.

Selected Bibliography

Bernstein, Morey, The Search for Bridey Murphey, Doubleday, New York 1965

James S Perkins, Experiencing Reincarnation, A Quest Book, 1977

Helen Wambach, Reliving Past Lives, Harper and Row, November 1978

Sutherland, Cherie, PhD, Transformed by the Light, Life After Near Death Experiences, Bantam Books, Australia, 1992

Helen Wambach, Life Before Life, Bantam Books, March 1979

Leslie D Weatherhead, The Case for Reincarnation, 1959

Ian Stevenson, European Cases of the Reincarnation Type, McFarland and Company, 2003. 270 pp. ISBN 0-7864-1458-8

Whitton, Dr Joel and Fisher, Joe, Life Between Life, Grafton Books, 1986

> "All faiths are inter-related and mutually indebted to each other, for the principles they teach and the disciplines they recommend are similar. The Vedic tradition is the first in Time. Buddhism, which appeared about 2500 years ago, is its son. Christianity, which was influenced by much in the Orient, is its grandson. Islam, which has the Prophets of Christianity as its base, is the great grandson. All have Love as the fundamental discipline of the mind in order to merge man with the Divine."
>
> Sathya Sai Baba

**The imposing
Statue of Christ
presiding over
the Hill-View
Stadium at
Prasanthi Nilayam**

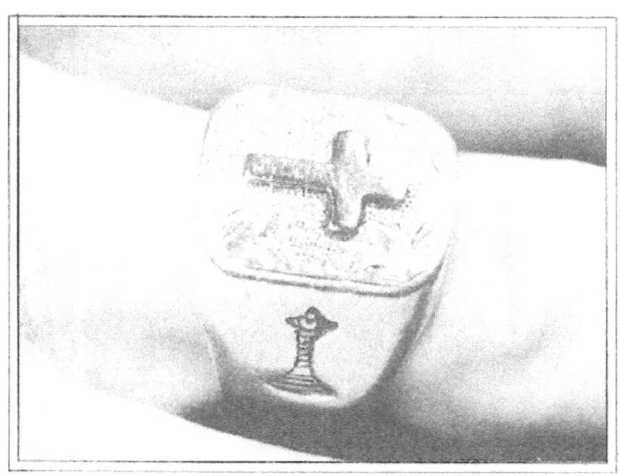

**The ring with a
Christian Cross
that Baba created
for Jason Peel**

CHAPTER ELEVEN

IMPLICATIONS OF SATHYA SAI BABA FOR THE CHURCH

"Jesus sacrificed His life for the regeneration and welfare of mankind Today, there are some who exaggerate the so-called differences between different faiths and, for their own selfish purposes, exploit these differences; they thereby bring a bad name to the founders of those religions, who were spiritual giants. No Prophet, or Messiah asked his followers to hate other religions or the followers of other faiths. Every religion has declared that God is One and that the Divine dwells in every being. Jesus also proclaimed the truth that the One Spirit resides in all beings."

Christianity has struggled long and hard to identify itself as the only true religion in a world of superstition. It has seen itself as a unique revelation of God, which is true. However, it is not the only valid revelation, and it does a gross disservice to all religion, as well as to God Himself in maintaining such exclusiveness. It has also prevented itself from enriching its understanding of God and His works by denying the validity of so much other evidence.

Christianity has generally concluded that if it is true and unique, then all other religions are false. This conclusion has led to effective separation from other spiritual traditions and to a backward-looking system becoming less relevant with the passage of time. Christianity has lost much of its spiritual power and influence by its claims to exclusivity.

The early Christians apparently expected Christ to return in their lifetime, which has been given as the reason for their not having committed their recollections of Christ's words and deeds to written form until many years after His disappearance.

For over two thousand years, Christians have been expecting the return of Christ. This expectation has been with them, apparently, from the time Christ disappeared from view. They have searched the Scriptures, particularly the Book of Revelation, for clues and while they have many ideas, they have no real certainty.

Christians admit that they do "not know the hour of His coming", nor the manner of His coming. From time to time someone sets a time for the coming of the Lord and the end of the world, which many believe will happen simultaneously. There are those who have ventured to set a date and time and who have waited in vain on mountain tops and caves at a predetermined time. Despite the warnings of Jesus about challenging times to come, they could not have foreseen just how dire the threats to humanity, and even the planet itself, would become.

There have been many false prophets over the centuries, and for this reason, Christians will take a lot of convincing to accept the Master when He does come. However, they should be prepared to consider how they will know when the true Christ is among us.

Revisions of History

It is to be hoped that in the Golden Age, the Church will be prepared to admit the errors of the past. History itself shows that the frantic clinging to increasingly tenuous positions means that the eventual and inevitable change of outlook becomes more embarrassing and humiliating when it does come. One has only to look at the Church's clinging to doctrines of the Flat Earth, the denial of Copernicus, the persecution of alleged witches and other errors, to see how the Church's credibility and authority is undermined by such absurdities.

The Church of Rome has within its vaults enough evidence of errors made many centuries ago for reasons of expediency, political requirements and other unworthy reasons, including sometimes ignorance and stupidity. Admittedly it is difficult to recant on these positions after having invoked Divine authority as sanctions, but the time is coming when such a change will inevitably happen.

The historical documents held in Rome should be available to scholars. While the Church clings to untruth, it will lack the authority of God and stunt the spiritual growth of its followers. In the Golden Age, there will be no place for continued deception and falsehood.

The early Church Councils, starting with the First Council of Nicaea, will need to be re-examined for the errors which were created to justify the power base of politically-minded men. In order to perpetuate the myths created in one generation, other myths had to be added. The Church will need to acknowledge that this actually happened. In the long run the Church will not lose out by admitting former errors and making amends by discovering for itself the essence of spirituality. This is what the Gospel is all about, anyway.

It will be better to do it sooner rather than leave it so late that it loses credibility as it did during the time of Copernicus.

Changes in Doctrine

Jesus was more concerned at changing the hearts of people than instructing them in doctrine. Spirituality, a matter for the heart, is stressed above doctrine, which a matter for the head. However, Man, being the intellectually curious creature that he is, has constructed theological and philosophical systems in an effort to explain the basic facts of Creation and Divinity. Christian doctrine is based upon the Bible, as interpreted by scholars and theologians. Because Paul was more concerned with doctrine than was Jesus, there is more arguably more emphasis upon the teachings of Paul in theology than those of Jesus. It is notable that disputes between Christians, as well as between Christians and members of other faiths, have usually been over doctrine rather than spirituality.

Inevitably, errors have arisen in Christian doctrine, some of which have proven destructive in the direction in which Christianity has been led.

The most pernicious mistake which many Christians make is to assume that belief in Jesus is sufficient for salvation, rather than the scrupulous application to His teachings -- despite Jesus' explicit statements to the contrary:

> *"Not everyone who says to me, 'Lord, Lord,' will enter the kingdom of heaven, but only the one who does the will of my Father in heaven. On that day many will say to me, 'Lord, Lord, did we not prophesy in your name, and cast out demons in your name, and do many deeds of power in your name?' Then I will declare to them, 'I never knew you; go away from me, you evil doers.'"*

> *"Everyone then who hears these words of mine and acts on them will be like a wise man who built his house on rock. The rain fell, the floods came and the winds blew and beat on that house. but it did not fall, because it had been founded on rock. And everyone who hears these words of mine an does not act on them will be like a foolish man who built his house on sand. The rain fell, and the floods came, and the winds blew and beat against that house, and it fell -- and great was its fall!"*
> *Matthew 7 : 21-23*

Too often the word "belief" is accepted as meaning "opinion" rather than being the fundamental basis of one's life. For this reason,

Christians have often been half-hearted and complacent about their faith, rather than *"with all their soul, and all their strength and all their mind"*. Belief without application of the principles is rather like a person who satisfies his hunger by reading a menu rather than eating the dinner!

Changes in Outlook

Christians may be expected to become less exclusive in outlook. The claim, long made by Christians that theirs is the only true religion will need to be revised.One of the ironies which Christians will find is that Christianity will be strengthened, not weakened when it is accepted as one revelation of God among others. The revelation of God through Jesus Christ is truly magnificent. He had an impact on the world which transcends the boundaries of Christianity. His sacrifice for the world had greater significance than even Christians can appreciate.

Changes in Scripture

The Bible, as we have it, is as much a political document as it is a spiritual one. The First Council of Nicaea established orthodoxy to suit the needs of the Emperor Constantine, encouraging some doctrines and suppressing others.

Many of the original documents of Christianity were destroyed by the early Church, particularly in the burning of the library at Alexandria. Others lie buried in the Vatican library in Rome.

References to India have been expurgated, hence the so-called *"missing years of Jesus"*, now accounted for in *"The Gospel of Saint Issa"*. Some documents may be restored to a place in the Bible. Other references which are in error should be removed.

A safe prophecy would be that within 100 years from now, there will be at least the beginnings of a new Christian Bible, much richer than the documents presently published, more convincing to the world and presenting a more credible account of the life and teachings of Jesus Christ.

As Christians realise their affinity with other spiritual traditions, they may be more prepared to accept as valid the Vedas of India, various Buddhist works, as well as the great body of teachings of Sathya Sai Baba.

> See yourself in all; love all as yourself. A dog caught in a room whose walls are mirrors sees in all the myriad which must be barked at. So it tires itself out by jumping on this reflection and that, and when the images also jump, it becomes mad with fury. The wise man, however, sees himself everywhere and is at peace; he is happy that there are so many reflections of himself all around him. That is the attitude you must learn to possess, that will save you from needless bother.
>
> Sathya Sai Baba

CHAPTER TWELVE

POSSIBLE OBJECTIONS BY CHRISTIANS

*"God sends sage~, saints and prophets to unveil the
Truth and Himself appears as an Avatar to awaken and
liberate mankind Iwo thousand years ago, when narrow
pride and ignorance defiled mankind, Jesus came as
the embodiment of Love and Compassion and lived
among men, holding forth the highest ideals of life."*

Sathya Sai Baba

Uniqueness of Jesus

An often-quoted verse raised in objection to the case for Sathya Sai
Baba as the Second Christ is Jesus's saying:

> *"I am the Way, the Truth and the Life. <u>No one comes to the
> Father but by Me"</u>.* John 14 : 6

I suspect that the underlined words are an addition to the words of
Jesus by a later scribe. In the prayer which Jesus gave us, He suggested
we address the Father directly, as in *"Our Father . . . "*. However, if He

actually said the words contained in this statement, Jesus would have been talking as the **Christ,** rather than as the **personality** of Jesus the man. Jesus later said *"I and the Father are One."* This means that when we come to Jesus we also come to the Father. It also means that when we come to the Father, we also come to Jesus.

Sathya Sai Baba has proclaimed Himself to be the Father, so we are now in the position of having direct access to the Father ourselves.

It may be that the statement of Jesus has been superseded by the Advent of Sathya Sai Baba, or more than likely, the statement attributed to Jesus was never said by Him. A scholar of the history of the New Testament will attest that some books of the New Testament were not compiled in their present form until many years (up to 100) after the Crucifixion, it is therefore quite likely that there are errors in recall or interpolations by others. The substantial differences between accounts of the same incidents in different Gospels indicates a wide margin of error in the accuracy of the New Testament.

Over the centuries, the Church has fostered the belief that only Christians have God's truth. This attitude has led to a high level of arrogance and intolerance among Christians, which has discredited Christianity in the eyes of many people. It also has lead to the rejection of the faith by many thinking, people.

To accept the Divinity of Christ is correct. It is correct to say that to live His teachings leads us to Salvation. It is also true that in Christ we have *"the Way, the Truth, and the Life."* However, it cannot be claimed that God has not **also** spoken to other people in their own way and according to their own needs. When the essential teachings of all religions are compared, there is a core of Universal truth which is more precious than differences in doctrine.

As Sathya Sai Baba says, no religion teaches people to speak falsely, live by hate and fail to restrain the senses. The Golden Rule is found in all major religions, expressed in various ways.

Sathya Sai Baba says repeatedly:

> *"There is only one caste, the caste of humanity. There is only one language, the language of the heart. There is only one religion, the religion of love. There is only one God, and He is omnipresent."*

Warnings of False Christs

Jesus warned us to beware of those coming in His name.

> *"For many shall come in My name, saying 'I am Christ' and shall deceive many."* Matthew 24 : 5

> *"For false Christs and false prophets shall rise and shall show signs and wonders, to seduce, if it were possible, even the elect."* Mark 13 : 22

It is true that in our time there have been many claimants to be the Christ or a special prophet. We need to be aware that any person who makes such a claim could be a deceiver. We also need to have some means of discriminating between the false Christs and the true One when we find Him.

Most claimants may be easily rejected by emphases such as bolstering their own egos, collecting money, sexually exploiting their followers, fomenting intolerance of others, persecution of those who depart from the "faith", or general lovelessness and other anti-spiritual attitudes.

The true Christ may be expected to represent Love in Action, to be a servant to all, be uninterested in money or personal power, to be free of ego, not given to anger, lust, greed, jealousy and other evils. The followers of the true Christ may be expected to seek to develop similar qualities in themselves, though not all will achieve them.

In the Introduction to this book two tests were given by which a claimant to Christhood may be assessed as to whether he may be the antichrist. The tests were that he would affirm the Divinity of the Father and the Son, and also that he would be acceptable to all faiths. Sathya Sai Baba passes both these tests.

However, it is most likely that the first reaction of many Christians on hearing of Sathya Sai Baba is that he must be the antichrist as prophesied in Scripture. This reaction must be faced. It is said *"You will know them by their fruits"* (Matthew 7 : 16, 20) and it has to be asserted that the fruits of Sathya Sai Baba are only positive and Divine.

Let us take a closer look at the meaning of the term antichrist and the authority for the idea. The biblical references to the antichrist are:

> *"Children, it is the last hour! As you have heard that antichrist is coming, so now many antichrists have come. From this we know that it is the last hour. They went out from us but they did not belong to us; for if they had belonged to us, they would have remained with us. But by going out they made it plain that none of them belongs to us. . . . . Who is the liar but the one who denies that Jesus is the Christ? This is the antichrist, the one who denies the Father and the Son. No one who denies the Son, has the Father."* I John 2: 18-23 (abridged)

> *"And every spirit that does not confess Jesus is not from God. And this is the spirit of the antichrist, of which you have heard that it is coming; and now is already in the world."* I John 4: 3

> *"Many deceivers have gone out into the world, those who do not confess that Jesus Christ has come in the flesh; any such person is the deceiver and an antichrist."* II John 7

In terms of John's descriptions, the world abounds with antichrists today, probably many more so than in the time the epistles were written.

However, by John's descriptions of the antichrist, Sathya Sai Baba clearly cannot be the antichrist, as Baba affirms the Divinity of Jesus, and enjoins Christians to follow the teachings of Jesus with all their heart, body, mind and soul.

Sathya Sai Baba seeks nothing for himself, does not seek converts for Himself, has no ambitions for Himself and teaches people that the greatest work that they can do is to serve other people for their sake. None of Baba's teachings would lead anyone to an act of violence, or hurt to another.

The objective of an antichrist is to increase the evil in the world, and lead Humanity into deeper darkness. This would happen through the denial of God and the Divinity of Jesus; the sowing of hatred, discord, division and immorality; and creating a climate of lawlessness, lovelessness and conflict in our society.

Rather than pointing the finger of suspicion on Sathya Sai Baba as the antichrist, should we not rather be looking to many of our political leaders, social agitators, and others who are actively, but usually unwittingly, furthering the objectives of the antichrist? Even some self-styled theologians who have no faith of their own, are actively undermining the faith of those who still believe in traditional Christianity. In our toleration and acceptance of such people we are aiding their mischief.

An antichrist would display none of the distinctive qualities of Sathya Sai Baba, who demonstrates the deepest love; teaches unity and faith in God; heals the sick in body, mind and spirit; and who reinforces the message of Jesus Christ.

One has only to read or hear Sathya Sai Baba expound on the teachings of Jesus to know that Jesus is being extolled and affirmed, rather than denied.There have been many Christians who have gone to Puttaparthi, where Sathya Sai Baba normally resides, to prove he is the Anti-Christ, and have come away with their hearts opened to a deeper, fuller, spiritual awareness and a personal feeling of having been privileged to experience God in person. It must be concluded that by all the accounts of the anti-Christ, it is not Sathya Sai Baba.

"People do not become wise by mere education. They are considering education as a means of livelihood rather than the art of living. The supreme goal of life should ever be kept in view. A small piece of fertile land is more valuable than a large tract of barren land; so also character is much more valuable and essential than scholarship. Today everybody is striving to acquire wealth, power and pelf which are like passing clouds while nobody bothers himself to acquire virtues which lead to the Truth Eternal. You must try to become exemplars of virtues, but not of wealth and power. It is a pity that even the elders who profess themselves to be well-wishers of society, are giving up their own ancient culture, lured by modernity. When the mother cow is grazing off the crop in the field, will its calf stand quiet on the field bund? It is impossible. It is no wonder the younger generation is following the bad example of their elders, leaders, parents and teachers who are not setting the right example for the youth to emulate. What is the reason for our ancients earning name and fame as upholders of morality in society? Because of their exemplary practice of virtues in daily life"

Sathya Sai Baba

The Crucifix that Baba materialised for Dr. Jack Hislop

Swami told him that it showed Christ as He really was at the time when He left His body. Baba said that the stomach is pulled in and the ribs all showing for Jesus had not eaten for eight days. Baba added that the wood is from the actual cross on which Christ was crucified and that it had taken a little time to find the wood after 2000 years. He said, "the image is of Christ after He died. It is a dead face."

Jack Hislop wondered about the hole showing at the top of the cross, and Baba explained that the cross had originally been hung from a standard, not let into the ground as has usually been depicted.

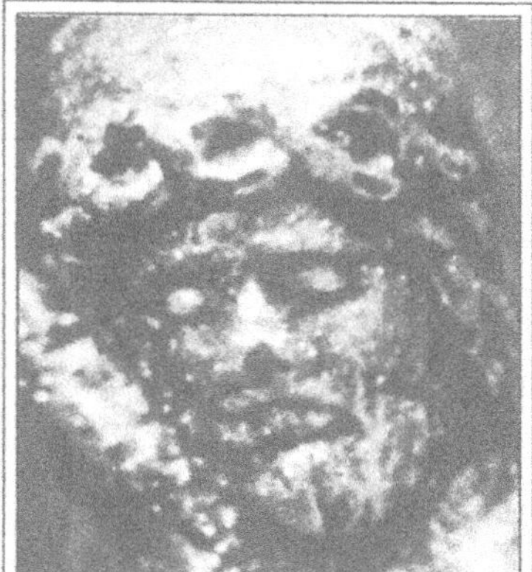

Detail of the face of Christ

CHAPTER THIRTEEN

CRIME AND CORRECTIONS

While Jesus was having dinner at Matthew's house, many tax collectors and sinners came and ate with him and his disciples. When the Pharisees saw this, they asked his disciples, "Why does your teacher eat with tax collectors and sinners?" On hearing this, Jesus said, "It is not the healthy who need a doctor, but the sick. But go and learn what this means: 'I desire mercy, not sacrifice. For I have not come to call the righteous, but sinners." (Matthew 9:10-14 (New International Version)

The age which is now concluding is based on many misconceptions and errors. Many of the greatest errors are based around our understanding of humanity and crime. In the Western world we have based social policies around the false beliefs that there are offenders and there are victims and that these are two distinct groups. This dichotomy creates a divide which is the cause of much social injustice.

In the course of my career I have been twice involved in the New Zealand Prison system, once as a prison psychologist (1962-65) and as a group facilitator with NZ Prison Fellowship at Rimutaka Prison (2003-2010). I have long considered that prisons are a waste of money and human life. They are generally based on false premises and represent belief that justice is served by treating people unjustly. A distinction is drawn between offenders and victims, ignoring the fact that offenders are usually victims of deprivation, poor parenting and verbal as well as physical abuse before they started offending.

Sai Baba had a demonstrated His Divine Powers in the miraculous events that occurred during my time at Rimutaka Prison. Appendix

Six is the transcription of a web page which may be found by a web search using *"Sai Baba Peter Phipps Prison Break."*

The lessons to be learned from the events are that God gives special grace to those we dismiss as *"rat-bags"* and rewards true repentance.

The account recorded in Appendix Six shows that:

1. Miracles can happen in the most unlikely of places;
2. It does not need a saint for God to respond with a miracle;
3. A sincere holy intention has great power;
4. Prayer and meditation can change the spiritual environment:
5. Anyone who sincerely repents can be transformed, whatever their faith or lack of faith.

Those we dismiss as the lowest in society may be the most spiritually discerning of all and find God within their hearts.

I have been told by some men that even the toughest of them will spend the night in bitter tears when they are first locked up at the beginning of a prison sentence. Several have reported to me that when they have reached the depths of despair that they may feel a comforting Presence in the cell and have even seen Jesus in a tangible form.

People who have suffered bereavement of someone very close to them may sometimes reach a similar level of despair and pain in which they experience a spirit of comfort.

At Rimutaka Prison miracles happened. Food and other substances were multiplied. Men were transformed. The Faith-Based model does work as Prison Fellowship has devised it, but it needs to be inter-faith. To assert that God works only through Christianity (or any other religion) is to diminish God and deny His Universality.

I would like to see almost every prison unit being faith-based and in this way make then into transformation centres rather than places of punishment. In this way the label of *"Corrections"* would become a reality, not a euphemism.

There will be some people who do not want transformation and for them the harshness of prison life would still be available.

It is my vision that such education should be available in the community as a resource to which probation officers and police could refer young offenders or youth at risk. Such community based facilities would be much cheaper and more effective than steel bars and razor-wire.

I am certain that in the near future the next incarnation of Sai Baba will use a similar program for the education and elevation of humanity.

In my country we are second only to the USA for incarcerating a large percentage of our populace. The budget for Corrections now exceeds the budget for education and is growing as a proportion of Government expenditure. This has become an unsustainable waste of resources and human life.

It is my sincere belief that anyone who applies the teachings of Sathya Sai Baba to develop a programme for the transformation of people we label as "criminals" will have positive results.

Swami has said that such projects should be privately funded as one cannot and should not rely on State resources. When the State is involved, a project is subject to bureaucratic and political interference as well as uncertainty of funding. All of Swami's projects are privately financed and use volunteers providing their skills as a service to God.

If such projects could start around the world, what is now seen as "the problem of crime" should be substantially reduced if not eliminated.

It is my prayer that this should happen if enough people are inspired to make it happen.

OM SAI RAM!

**Sathya Sai College of Arts, Science and Commerce
at Whitefield, Bangalore**

Sathya Sai Arts and Science College for women at Anantapur

CHAPTER FOURTEEN

THE TRIPLE INCARNATION OF SAI BABA

In the first edition of this book I refrained from mentioning the Triple Incarnation (as devotees call it) of Sai Baba. My reason was that on hearing about Sai Baba, a Christian has many issues to face before acceptance. Reincarnation is one of the major issues, which has been covered in an earlier chapter. The issue to be tackled in this chapter is why, where Jesus needed only three years to change the direction of human history, a later coming of the Cosmic Christ would need three lifetimes, covering nearly 300 years, to complete the task. A complete answer to this question is beyond the scope of this work, but I provide a few points in this chapter.

I am also raising the issue of the Triple Incarnation because there is greater urgency in getting out the message of what God is doing to save humanity form the dire threats to our very existence in the form of nuclear war and choking pollution. We are also under threat from corporations wishing to take over our food supplies, natural resources, health care and land. Governments are making laws to take away our freedom under the guise of protecting our security.

It is said that currently a group of less than one percent of the people of the world own 82 percent of the world's resources. This is behind most of the world's poverty and is a major cause of crime in the world. Swami said that the trouble the world is that money is in the wrong hands and He has to fix this.

The First Incarnation: Sai Baba of Shirdi

Shirdi Sai Baba probably took birth near the village of Shirdi in the Ahmednagar district of Maharashtra around the year 1838 He alternated between sleeping in a Hindu temple one night and a Moslem mosque the next.

He was accepted as a saint by both Hindu and Moslem people. He was known for many miracles. He taught, as Sathya Sai Baba did later, to love all beings without discrimination, to study the scriptures of one=s faith while acknowledging the value of other faiths. He was particularly concerned to bridge the gap between Hindus and Moslems. People of other faiths were also drawn to his circle. In Wikipedia it is reported A*People coming to his abode were so taken aback to see Hindus, Muslims, and others living together so peacefully that in many instances it changed their entire lives and belief systems@*

Before Shirdi Sai Baba entered Mahasamadhi in 1918 He prophesied that He would take birth again in eight years.

The Second Incarnation: Sathya Sai Baba

Sathya Sai Baba took birth in the village of Puttaparthi in 1926 as the Second Incarnation. Some of His Life has already been documented in the present book. His departure from that embodiment is described in Appendix Five by Lyn Kriegler.Sathya Sai Baba established a system of education based on spiritual principles. He said that while a being such as Rabindranath Tagore (1861-1941) normally arises once in several generations, as a result of Sathya Sai education there will be hundreds of people of the great calibre of Tagore coming out of His universities. There are now some thousands of graduates of Swami's universities making their way into the fields of science, government, commerce and management. These people will have an enormous impact on the world.

It would be a mistake to assume that just because Swami no longer has an identifiable physical form that He no longer is able to influence people or world events. Before the advent of the Third Incarnation: Prema Sai Baba.

Swami frequently mentioned that as Sai Baba of Shirdi His Mission was to prepare for the great changes which are to come to humanity. He explained His connection with previous Divine Incarnations, including Jesus, Shiva, Krishna, and others. He referred to His future Incarnation as Prema Sai Baba. He likened the three stages to a host preparing a banquet. Shirdi Sai Baba was preparing the ingredients for the meal, Sathya Sai Baba was cooking the food, and with Prema Sai Baba we shall all be able to enjoy the meal together.

Swami also used another analogy in relation to the feminine and masculine principles, in that God has both masculine and feminine aspects. In previous Divine Incarnations, Shiva was a powerful, judgmental figure; while His consort, Shakti was a loving, sweet-natured person. Krishna destroyed armies to rid the planet of evil; while His consort, Radha was the feminine, loving aspect. Jesus was capable of wrath, as when threw the bankers out of the temple and heavily criticised the Pharisees,

While Mary Magdalene provided a loving, caring aspect. Swami said that as Sai Baba of Shirdi, He was Shiva. As Sathya Sai Baba He was both Shiva and Shakti at different times and places. I have witnessed this myself. At His ashram at Puttaparthi He was often stern, judgmental and critical. At His ashram at Brindavan, He was softer, sweeter and more loving.

Swami has said that in His third Incarnation as Prema Sai Baba He will be purely Shakti (feminine qualities), gentle and loving. There is some way to go before the world is ready for the Incarnation of Love. Swami said that as Sai Baba of Shirdi, He was Shiva. As Sathya Sai Baba He was both Shiva and Shakti at different times and places. I have witnessed this myself.

At His ashram at Puttaparthi He was often stern, judgmental and critical. At His ashram at Brindavan, He was softer, sweeter and more loving.

Swami has said that in His third Incarnation as Prema Sai Baba He will be purely Shakti (feminine qualities), gentle and loving. There is some way to go before the world is ready for the Incarnation of Love.

Final Days and Physical Passing (Mahasamadhi) of Bhagavan Sri Sathya Baba (Written by Lyn Kriegler)

Easter Sunday morning, April 24, 2011 began like any other interlude where Sathya Sai Baba appeared to be unwell. Throughout His life there had been many incidents where He appeared to be unwell, taking on the appearance of a stroke victim, the fracturing of His hip due to a fall in His later years, trance-like states during which, He would later stateChad gone to the rescue of a devotee suffering from a devastating ailment or life-threatening condition. He spoke freely of these events and the fact that it was purely out of love that He performed these miraculous healings and resurrections.

During March of 2011 Swami>s doctors announced that He had been admitted to the Institute of Higher Medical Sciences at Prashantigram. This is the famed ASuperhospital", one of two world-class super speciality hospital facilities in India founded by Sathya Sai Baba. (The other Superhospital is located in Bangalore).

The doctors issued daily reports on Swami>s condition. He was on dialysis. He was being treated for an infection. He was on a ventilator. At first the reports seemed positive. Swami was lucid; He was interacting with the doctors and members of his family. A few much loved staff members were permitted to wait outside his room, hoping and praying that this was just another event that Swami would Acome back@ from.

As March segued into April, the reports became more sombre. Swami appeared to be in a coma. There were signs of organ failure. The stress was beginning to show amongst doctors and hospital staff as the inevitable became more and more of a possibility.

Finally in the early hours of Easter Sunday, no pulse or signs of life were detected. The Divine Form beloved by untold numbers of followers worldwide had taken Mahasamadhi (Final release from the body by a holy being). Swami's body was transported by ambulance to Sai Kulwant Hall in His main ashram Prashanti Nilayam. Hundreds of devotees were gathered there for morning chanting and bhajan. Swami>s translator Professor Anil Kumar stepped up to the microphone to make the official announcement: the being known to millions as Bhagavan Sathya Sai Baba was no more.

The outpouring of grief was uncontrollable and unimaginable as thousands flocked to the ashram for the services held over the following days. Heads of state including the Prime Minister of India, the President of India, state ministers, governors, representatives from the India>s armed forces, sports luminaries and ordinary people from near and far travelled to attend the final rites.

A guard of honour was placed around the glass enclosed casket draped with the flag of India. Hindu priests, Buddhist monks, a Christian minister, representatives from the Muslim world and other faiths offered prayers and spoke of the unparalleled achievements and contributions of selfless love and service that were the hallmark of Swami>s long life.

The Third Incarnation: Prema Sai Baba

Swami frequently mentioned that as Sai Baba of Shirdi His Mission was to prepare for the great changes which are to come to humanity.

He explained His connection with previous Divine Incarnations, including Jesus, Shiva, Krishna, and others. He referred to His future Incarnation as Prema Sai Baba. He likened the three stages to a host preparing a banquet. Shirdi Sai Baba was preparing the ingredients for the the meal, Sathya Sai Baba was cooking the food, and with Prema Sai Baba we shall all be able to enjoy the meal together.

He also used another analogy in relation to the feminine and masculine principles, in that God has both masculine and feminine aspects. In previous Divine Incarnations, Shiva was a powerful, judgmental figure; while His consort, Shakti was a loving, sweet-natured person. Krishna destroyed armies to rid the planet of evil; while His consort, Radha was the feminine, loving aspect. Jesus was capable of wrath, as when threw the bankers out of the temple and heavily criticised the Pharisees, while Mary Magdalene provided a loving, caring aspect.

Swami said that as Sai Baba of Shirdi, He was Shiva As Sathya Sai Baba He was both Shiva and Shakti at different times and places. I have witnessed this myself. At His ashram at Puttaparthi He was often stern, judgmental and critical. At His ashram at Brindavan, He was softer, sweeter and more loving.

Swami has said that in His third Incarnation as Prema Sai Baba He will be purely Shakti, gentle and loving.

The Interregnum

Before the Incarnation of Prema Sai Baba can occur, the work of Sathya Sai Baba must be completed. It is noted that ASathya@ means Truth. While in common usage, Atruth@ means Afactually correct@, in reality it has connotations of Arighteousness@, Asteadfastness@, Ahonesty@ and Avirtue@.

The following Bible verse conveys a good example of the full meaning of Truth:

AOnly fear the LORD, and serve him in truth with all your heart: for consider how great things he hath done for you,@ (1 Samuel 12:24)

Another example:

AAnd the Word was made flesh, and dwelt among us, (and we beheld his glory, the glory as of the only begotten of the Father,) full of grace and truth.@ (John 1:14)

In the Bible there are references to Athe Spirit of Truth@ which I believe refers to Sathya Sai Baba. Consider the following verse:

Howbeit when he, the Spirit of truth, is come, he will guide you into all truth: for he shall not speak of himself; but whatsoever he shall hear, that shall he speak: and he will show you things to come.

Other verses worth consulting are Romans 2:2, Romans 2:8, Romans 2:20, Colossians 1:5

Where there is Truth, there are other Divine qualities such as Justice, Peace, and Right Conduct. In a world where Truth is supreme, there will be no fear, terrorism and crime. The Coming Golden Age will be a world of Truth and we are yet to see its fulfilment. However, we can see the start of it in the present time.

At the time of writing (2018) there is a massive spiritual battle between the forces of Truth and Evil, and it appears that Truth is at last winning. For too long we had become accustomed to believing that wars are inevitable, the strong can oppress the weak, the Aweak get richer and the poor get poorer@, politicians can ignore their election promises once elected, and poverty is inevitable. We have seen bankers profiting from war by funding both sides of a conflict and industrialists amass immense wealth by producing the weapons of war.

We have seen the planet being destroyed in the name of "progress" by corporations who seize irreplaceable mineral assets for the sake of short terms profits. Those who have power and wealth have literally got away with murder as they declare themselves above the law. Bankers who have made foolish investment decisions and incurred massive losses are reimbursed by taxpayers as the banks are *"too big to fail"*.

For a long time we have lived with the threat of a nuclear holocaust, where one mad dictator on any side could launch an attack on another state, which could lead to a world-wide exchange of nuclear weapons and the destruction of all life on earth. Swami has promised us that such an event will not happen, but we shall all be more secure when nuclear weapons are abandoned.

As individuals we have felt powerless to make any difference to what is a corrupt and ruthless world system. It will literally take an Act of God to change the system, and we may be assured that this will happen. It is why Sai Baba has come to us.

Now we can see a reversal of the power structure of the world. People are now more aware of corruption and injustice in the world and are less tolerant. Politicians and corporate leaders are being held to account for their crimes.

It would be a gross error to assume that because the "Spirit of Truth" does not have an identifiable physical form He is absent or not effective. Apart from His legacy in the form of thousands of graduates from His education system, and many millions of devotees quietly living as He directed, He has appeared in physical form to many people since His departure from His body. The work of the Spirit of Truth does not end.

We are reminded of the declaration of Krishna, where in the Bhagavad Gita, He says:

> *Whenever righteousness wanes and unrighteousness increases I send myself forth.*
> *For the protection of the good and for the destruction of evil, and for the establishment of righteousness,*
> *I come into being age after age.*

—Bhagavad Gita 4.7–8

We now await and prepare for the Advent of the Spirit of Love in Prema Sai Baba

POSTSCRIPT TO SECOND EDITION

Reading through the first edition I realize that my estimate of time scales was most inaccurate. A quarter century ago few of us realized the depths of depravity, corruption and evil which the Lord would have to deal with before His Kingdom could be re-established. But I am certain that the time will soon be here when corruption will be overthrown.

I have used the title *"A Gospel for the Golden Age"* which has caused some comments, as it may seem pretentious. In using the term *"Gospel"*, I am not claiming the story to be a dogma (as has been suggested) or to be the only story. There will be many other gospels in time to come. Christians often define "Gospel" as Good News. This has been my intention in using the word in the current context. I am not claiming equality with the four apostles of Jesus (Matthew, Mark, Luke and John). My intention has been simply to tell a story as simply as I could of a Divine Being comparable with Jesus Christ.

While every book by its nature has a beginning, a middle and an end, a book must always be a work in progress. There is certainly no end to the stories that have yet to be written about Sai Baba. Swami frequently said though we might study Him for a thousand years, we will never understand Him. He is beyond human comprehension.

He once said that he is aware of every blade of grass blowing in the wind. I once looked at a hillside covered with grass and thought of all the hillsides and plains of the world and wondered about the Mind that can be aware of each blade at the same time. Such a Mind is beyond our understanding. I then thought of the findings of cosmologists. We are told that there are 200 to 400 billion stars in our galaxy that we call the Milky Way.

How many paddocks are on the planets associated with those stars? We are told there are 200 to 400 billion galaxies in the Universe. There is no way the human mind can grasp those numbers. How can we understand a God who has in mind at the same time every blade of grass, every living being and every rock on every world? Our intellect can never approach such an understanding. Our theologies cannot come close to understanding God.

God can be understood only through the heart, through our love, our devotion to Him. In the Christmas discourse of 1963, Swami said:

> *Bhakthi (devotion) involves dedication with nothing held back, not even a wisp of ego should remain. His command alone counts, His Will prevails. Like a drunkard, the Bhaktha (devotee) has no sense of honor or decency, pride or conceit. He is a mad person, unconcerned with all that is unrelated to his ideal. He is deaf to the call of hunger and thirst, he misses steps in logic and he calculates wrongly while dealing in the market place. Narada (a Vedic sage) says that those full of the liquor of ignorance stumble after the shadows of the world, while those drunk with the nectar of wisdom never move away from the Highest, which they have discovered as themselves.*

Swami ended the discourse:

> *Be confident that you will be liberated. Know that you are saved. Go and tell all that you had gone to Puttaparthi and that you got there the secret of liberation.*

Sai Baba does not intend to start a new religion or to challenge any faith. He is not a threat to any religion. Religions have value in pointing the way to God and minding the sacred texts, but God is beyond any religion.

The children on stage with Swami

Sathya Sai Baba joining the international caste of children for the finale of one of the Christmas Plays held annually at Prasanthi Nilayam

Christ and His disciples on the Sea of Galilee

Children enacting an episode from the life of Jesus during the Christmas Play in 1991

APPENDICES

Introduction

I am aware that many readers will be trying to put holes in the arguments presented in this book. I have been through the same process myself. Were there only one or two testimonies to the Divinity of Sathya Sai Baba, then they can be dismissed as fiction or delusion. When, however, there is a large body of testimony from many sane and intelligent people, all consistent in their story, then it becomes harder to dismiss the accounts.

Trying to disprove Sathya Sai Baba is rather like the Uncle Remus story of wrestling with the tar baby. The more you try to fight Him, the more involved one becomes. He welcomes such testing, for out of the struggle comes conviction of the Truth.

I read many such accounts such as the ones appended, looking for contradictions, signs of pathology, charlatanism or fraud. There were a few minor contradictions, but the overwhelming consistency of accounts from many people was more impressive. The final step for me was to visit Prasanthi Nilayam and see Sathya Sai Baba in the flesh, as well as to talk to many devotees with personal testimonies and thrilling experiences.

The appendices were selected to provide a taste of the accounts of works of Sathya Sai Baba. It is hoped that the taste will stimulate the reader to read more widely among the many books available. There are countless numbers of similar accounts available in the literature and still many more personal experiences of devotees shared in sath-sanga, (discussions of the Glories of the Lord) which, despite the diversity, show a common theme.

The balance of evidence must lead, in my view, to only one conclusion, that Sathya Sai Baba is indeed the Lord incarnated in our time. The following appendices present a mere fraction of some of the available writings about Sathya Sai Baba.

Appendix 1 is from Mr Ron Laing, a Briton who has written a series of papers about Sathya Sai Baba, which are collected together in a book co-authored with his wife, Peggy Mason, and entitled "Embodiment of Love".

Appendix 2 is an account of the resurrection from the dead of Walter Cowan. This is perhaps the best known of the accounts of Sathya Sai Baba raising the dead, but there are many more examples of what we have come to call "miracles".

Appendix 3 is the account of Joel Riordan, whose amusing first encounter with Baba is well known in Sai Baba circles.

Appendix 4 is from a prominent Baptist minister in the USA, the Rev Robert Earl Pipes. This paper was in the version of a draft which I sent to Prasanthi Nilayam, in the care of a most gracious devotee by the name of Mata Betty, to obtain Swami's blessing on the project, if He so willed. After the book had been sent, I revised the contents of the book and decided to omit the paper by Mr Pipes, so my draft becoming ready for publication was then not the same as that presented to Swami.

When Baba was shown the book, he asked for the name and, on being told the title said "Oh yes, by Peter Phipes". Mata Betty was puzzled by the pronunciation. When this response was conveyed to myself, I knew immediately that Swami wanted "Pipes" to be included with "Phipps". Such a witty response containing both humor and a direction, showing knowledge of the book and its contents, as well as my intentions, was made without having touched the book physically or had a chance to see inside the covers by means which we regard as normal. By the change of one syllable of one word, Swami confirmed knowledge and approval of the project. He later blessed the book itself.

> "Knowledge that does not give harmony and wholeness to the process of living, is not worth acquiring. Every activity must be rendered valid and worth-while by its contribution to the discovery of Truth, both of the Self and of Nature. Of what use is it to know everything about Nature, if you do not know anything of the Self! Nature is only a projection of the Self, therefore, unless the Self is known, knowledge of Nature is either distorted or deceptive. The Self is Atma, of which the entire Creation is composed, so knowledge of the Self alone can quench the thirst of man."
>
> Sathya Sai Baba

APPENDIX 1

THE SECOND COMING HAS COME!

Mr. Ron Laing is deeply interested in spirituality and is a well-known writer on supernormal phenomena. He has written for various journals including Psychic News, published in the U.K., for many years. He is a devout Christian and has recognised in Bhagavan the manifestation of the Cosmic Christ. He writes:

I have studied the life and teachings of Sathya Sai Baba for two years, and I have no doubt whatever that once again we have 'the Word made flesh' on earth, the Divine Principle incarnate - indeed an Avatar who has come to save the world from destruction and to usher in a new Golden Age. As a matter of fact, I sensed with a kind of soul-sight after reading no more than ten pages of the first book I read, and I have been increasingly overwhelmed by the impact since that first magic moment. Sai Baba says:

> *'I shall not fail; it is not in the nature of Avatars to fail. Mankind will be saved and a new Golden Age will recur.'*

But what has impacted me equally is the extraordinary similarity in the life, teachings and personality of Sathya Sai Baba and the Christ, not only in the basic tenets but in the specific detail in which both express themselves in words and phraseology which are virtually identical. This is simply not so if you study the sayings of Krishna, the Buddha, Mahomet, or any other founder of a world religion. Of course it is true that all world religions basically assert the same truths, but there is an extraordinary identity between Sai Baba and the Christ which is quite unique.

The Christ said through Jesus of Nazareth:

"I am the Way, the Truth, and the Life. The Father and I are one; no one comes to the Father except through me."

On the face of it this incredible statement must, in essence, either be true, or the hallucination of the biggest megalomaniac of his time. Now the teachings of a megalomaniac do not survive for 2,000 years. Falsity can deceive for a time, but it cannot survive for centuries unless it has at least a basis of truth in it. As the poet, William Platt put it: *"That which has life shall surely live forever; only that dies which was forever dead"*. The fact remains that the Christ's teachings and life have inspired saints and martyrs throughout history to follow his teaching and example.

Sathya Sai Baba has made even more incredible statements:

"My power is immeasurable, my truth is inexplicable, unfathomable. I am beyond the reach of the most intensive enquiry and the most meticulous measurement. There is nothing I do not see, nowhere I do not know the way, no problem I cannot solve. My sufficiency is unconditional. I am the totality - all of it."

Megalomania? Yet in a mere forty years since his mission started this man has gathered around him 50 million devotees in India, has 3,000 Sai centres in that continent, and has built five Colleges. His fame is now worldwide, despite shunning publicity; there are centres in virtually every country in the Western world. He is probably better known in India, in the real sense, than the Pope is in Europe.

The teaching of both Jesus Christ and Sathya Sai Baba is exoteric and esoteric. Christ taught the masses in simple parables, yet astounded the scholars and theologians in the Temple with the scope of his knowledge and the depth of his perception. Baba also teaches the masses in parables, yet he can explain the most abstruse mysteries of the Vedas to India's pundits.

Both come over as Men of the People, intensely human and lovable, albeit Divine, rather than as cloistered Holy Men. One feels this about the Christ, at one and the same time a friend and a God-man. Christ commanded an audience no doubt of thousands during his Sermon on the Mount, and was acclaimed by virtually the entire city on his entry into Jerusalem. Baba commands an audience of tens of thousands (up to a quarter of a million) during Festivals when he gives Darshan or on a whirlwind visit to a big city.

Both started their missions when children. Christ taught in the Temple at Jerusalem at the age of twelve. Baba was performing miracles at the age of eight and started his mission at the age of thirteen.

The basic aims and tenets of faith of both are the same. The Christ did not intend to start a new religion. He came to fulfil the Law of One and proclaim new revelation, to build on the old, to stop malpractices such as animal sacrifice, to end the corruption, to point out the errors in the Scriptures, to amend the old law of an eye for an eye and a tooth for a tooth with the precept to love one's enemies and to turn the other cheek.

Neither is Sai Baba founding a new religion. He is continually re-energising old shrines, and pointing out the interpolations, excisions and misinterpretations of the Vedas to India's Vedic scholars. As he says: *"I have come to repair the ancient Highway to God"*. One might say there is nothing new under the spiritual sun.

Christ upheld the role of women and tried to raise their status above the level of mere chattels at a time when men doubted if women had souls. He was often surrounded by women, not only his mother, but Mary and Martha and Mary Magdalene who were all devoted to him. Sai Baba declares: *"Woman is equally equipped with man to tread the spiritual path."* He elevates women in their vital role of motherhood as being the custodians of future generations. His first College was built solely for the education of women.

But of course the cornerstone of the teaching of these two God-men can be summed up in the one word, Love. No newcomer to the Gospels, unconditioned by theology, could possibly read them without gaining the overwhelming impression that the paramount message contained therein is one of Love.

> *"Love God, and thy neighbor as thyself, and on these two commandments hang all the laws and the prophets."*

It is the golden rule to live by, the criterion to apply to every decision and to every judgement. Sai Baba, too, is the embodiment of Love. It is the essence of all his teaching.

> *"Start the day with love, fill the day with love, end the day with love - this is the quickest and most direct way to God. Most routes are circuitous, but the direct path is Love. Other paths develop conceit, separate man from man, separate man from beast. They contract, they do not reach out; they shrink your awareness of the Divine. My teaching is Prema (Love), my activity is Prema, my instrument is Prema, my way of life is Prema. There is nothing more precious within human grasp than Love."*

As with the teachings, so with the personalities and miracles. It is clear that Christ had a radiant transparency, a Divine charisma, with no trace of affectation, of pride and ego and that He was motivated solely by Love, with love literally radiating from him. The impact of meeting him must have been soul-shattering. How else could a man walk up to a small group of illiterate fishermen, chat to them for an hour, and then say, *"follow Me,"* and have them do just that, abandoning all? Sai Baba has a similar effect. The sight of him changes people. Often souls are transformed instantly.

One gets the impression that Christ preferred simple people and the simple life; in the main he chose simple folk as his disciples. Baba often rails at the scholars and pedants, with their 'desire for disputation and the laurels of victory over those preening themselves as learned.' *"Be simple and sincere"*, he tells his devotees. Both show a dislike of the Pharisee type. Christ called them 'whited sepulchres'. Swami calls them 'dry as dust scholars exulting in their casuistry and argumentative skills'.

In contrast both have clearly shown their love of children. Christ upbraided his disciples *"Suffer little children to come unto me."* Baba shares a similar love. The daughter of the Leader of the Sai Centre in Wellingborough escorted a group of children to Puttaparthi in the summer of 1978. The children took with them seven sacks of presents for Swami, containing everything from a large teddy-bear to a packet of Weetabix! Baba insisted on personally inspecting every single item, expressing his delight according to the degree of love with which he was able to sense the gift had been made. He adored them, and spent hours with them while important functionaries were awaiting an interview.

Of course both have been maligned and persecuted. *"Calumny is the lot of all great souls everywhere, at any time."* Baba says he is oblivious to praise or blame. Christ was accused of being a wine-bibber, and of mixing with publicans and sinners. Baba has been criticised for allowing sinners to use the Ashram at Puttaparthi. Their replies were similar:

Jesus: *"I am come to recall the sinners, not the righteous."*

Baba replied: *"Sinners have more need of me than you have."*

Christ was accused of healing by the powers of Satan (Beelzebub). Baba has been denounced as a black magician. He has been accused of having a luxurious taste in dress. (He actually wears plain cotton robes). His reply: *"Would I be holier in rags?"*

But the most significant thing about the miracles of Sai Baba is when he has identified himself with the Christ. He has given a detailed account of the life and journeyings of Christ from the age of 12 to 30 to fill the gap in the Gospels, and from this account a film has been made by Richard Bock in California. Christmas itself is regarded as a Festival at the Ashram and celebrated with great fervour - in fact more so than in the West where it has become so grossly commercialised. Baba often gives talks to small groups of Christians and points out the excisions and interpolations in the Gospels. To those who feel a sense of disloyalty to Christianity he has on more than one occasion manifested a figure of Christ above his head, thus identifying the two. There are also accounts of people praying before a statue of Christ and seeing it transform into an image of Sai Baba.

Dr. John Hislop recounts how, when he was walking one day with Baba, he took two twigs from a tree, placed them into a cross, blew on them three times and transformed them into a cross with a silver statue of Jesus on it, explaining that the likeness was an exact replica of the likeness of Jesus as he was on the cross! There was a small hole at the top of the upright, and when questioned about this Baba said that the cross on which Jesus was crucified was hung on a pole and not put into the ground. The magnified photograph shows a face not unlike Baba's, strong in character, but gnarled with sweat, blood and the hallmark of agony. The ribs are bare from lack of food. Blood can be seen flowing from the forehead, and black, dust-caked saliva at the corner of the mouth. There is a haunting expression of agony in the eyes.

One day when a group were looking at this crucifix in Dr. Hislop's home in California, a strong wind suddenly blew up and there was a crash of thunder from skies which were perfectly clear. This 'mystery' was reported in the local San Diego Tribune the following day, confirming that the skies were clear. It happened at 5 pm. which scholars believe was the approximate time of Christ's death when similar thunder broke out and the Temple veil was said to have been riven!

Finally, on Christmas Day, 1972, Baba referred to Jesus's statement, *"He who has sent me will come again"*, and then made the astonishing claim that Jesus was referring to himself, Baba. Although expunged from the Bible, Baba claims that Jesus's words were: *"His name will be Truth. He will wear a red robe. He will be short, with a crown of hair."* "Sathya" means Truth. Baba wears a red robe, is short, and has a crown of hair.

In January 1980, my wife and I flew to India to visit the Ashram at Brindavan. To our utter astonishment we received the incomparable blessing of four interviews (three private and one group) in less than a fortnight. On the 19th of January we were taken into Swami's inner sanctum and sat with him entirely alone. I picked up every vestige of courage that was in me and referred to Baba's statement on Christmas Day 1972.

I said: *"Swami, does this omission in the Bible mean that it was You who sent Jesus of Nazareth into incarnation?"*

"Yes," he replied.

My wife said I gasped, although I have no recollection of this. Followed my final question which lay at the very core of my soul: *"In that case, are You what Western Christians call the Cosmic Christ?"*

"Yes," He said again.

It is impossible to convey in words the tone, the quiet assurance, in which he affirmed these two questions. Gently, lovingly, with total conviction, with a sort of ineffable simplicity, and perhaps most important of all, with a total lack of self-consciousness impossible in a mere human, he looked straight into my eyes which were no more than twelve inches from his, and just said *"Yes."* I only know that it was impossible not to believe him.

As the reader can imagine, my wife and I came out of that interview in a daze. So Sathya Sai Baba was the One whom Jesus called the Father, the Christ, indeed the Cosmic Christ! The Second Coming had come, had lived for fifty-four years, and perhaps only a handful of Christians were aware of the fact! At first it was too stupendous to grasp. Yet I only know that I came to believe it, and that I am reporting precisely what occurred.

> Abridged from the book "Embodiment of Love" by Peggy Mason and Ron Laing, published by Gateway Books, The Hollies, Wellow, Bath, BA2 8QJ

APPENDIX 2

THE RESURRECTION OF WALTER COWAN

This is taken from Dr. John S. Hislop's well-known book, "My Baba and I". Dr. Hislop is a long-standing devotee of Sathya Sai Baba, he and his wife having first some to Baba in 1968. Over the years, he has had the privilege of spending a lot of time in Baba's company, frequently travelling with him in the same car, and has been granted countless interviews. Many years ago, Baba gave him the job of starting the first Sai Centre in America and he was President of the Sathya Sai Council of America for many years.

Resurrection, the rising again from the dead, is something which all Christians have heard of, and because it is a sacred story we tend to believe it -- if we have not been pounded by doubts from agnostics, atheists, humanists, and people who, in general, hold to reason and logic more than to faith. And, stories of resurrection in recent times come from people who are not viewed as "establishment" and the stories are not, therefore, given serious attention. Mostly, what has been said above refers to the western world. The same structure of belief and disbelief about resurrection is not the norm in India, and this story is about events which occurred in India, although Walter Cowan and myself were born in the West.

Walter died in his room at the Connemara Hotel in Madras. He and his wife, Elsie, had arrived there on December 23, 1971 to see Baba, who himself was in Madras to preside at an All-India Conference of Sai Organizations.

Early on the morning of December 25, a rumour quickly spread that an elderly American had died of a heart attack. My wife, Victoria and

I immediately thought of Walter. We went to the hotel and found Elsie there. Walter had fallen to the floor in the very early morning hours. Elsie had called Mrs. Ratanlal whose room was just down the corridor. The two women managed to lift Walter to the bed, and he passed away in Elsie's arms a few minutes later. An ambulance was called, the body was taken to hospital, pronounced dead upon arrival, placed in an empty storage room, and covered with a sheet to await daylight and decisions about the funeral.

Elsie and Mrs. Ratanlal had already been to see Baba when we arrived. He had told them he would visit the hospital at 10 a.m. The two ladies were ready and waiting to join Baba at the appointed hour. They did go to the hospital, but Baba had arrived earlier and had already departed. To the joy of the ladies, but also to their total amazement, they found Walter alive and being attended to. Nobody saw Baba with Walter, nor has Baba chosen to say how or why Walter was resurrected, but on returning to the devotee family who were his hosts, Baba told the people there that he had brought Walter back to life.

Walter's own story throws some light on what happened, and later on, I was a party to a fascinating episode; for Walter's life continued to be in danger and, in fact, Baba told me that Walter died three times and had to be returned to life three times.

Walter described his experience. He said he realized that he had died and that he had remained with the body in the ambulance, looking at it with interest. Then Baba came and together they went to a place, which seemed to be at a great height. There they entered a conference room where people were seated around a table. There was a presiding chairman who had a kind face and who spoke in a kindly way. He called for Walter's records and these were read aloud. The records were in different languages and Walter did not understand what was said until after some time when Baba started to translate. Walter was surprised to hear that he had occupied a lofty status in various times and cultures and had always been dedicated to the welfare of the people. At length, Baba addressed the person presiding and asked that Walter be given over to Baba's care, for Baba had work for Walter to do. Then, when Baba and he departed the room, Walter felt himself descending towards a place where his body was, but felt great reluctance. In terms of direct experience, he had realized that he was not the body, and he had no wish to be subject again to bodily anxieties and miseries.

After hearing Walter, I asked Baba if Walter were just imagining the incidents. Baba replied that it was not imagination. The events were real. They had occurred in Walter's mind and Baba himself had guided the thoughts. I then asked if everyone had a similar experience at death. Baba answered that some people had similar experiences and some did not. Several years later I brought up the question again. Baba answered that the corpse was common to all, but beyond that there was no common experience.

The day after Walter returned to life was one of high interest for me. Sri Appa and I accompanied Baba to the home of a devotee. From there we went to a meeting of lady members of the Nigara Sai Samiti where Baba was to give awards and speak. Sri Appa and I were sitting on the platform, just a few feet from Baba, and were able to observe him closely. He made the awards and gave a spiritual discourse, all without any break or any moment of hesitation. From that meeting, we were to go to the home of a devotee for lunch. As soon as we got in the car, Baba turned to us and said, *"While I was talking in the meeting, Mrs. Cowan called me. I at once went to the hospital and did what was necessary. Mr. Cowan's health had taken a bad turn for the worse."*

So, even while busy on the speaker's platform, Baba had gone to the hospital, and had done what was necessary. But, to the eyes of Sri Appa and myself, Baba had continued in action and speech on the platform for the whole time without any break or hesitation whatsoever. How does one explain this mystery?

When we arrived at the devotee's house for lunch, Baba turned to us and said, "You will not be able to join me for lunch. Take this vibhuthi to the hospital, give Mr. Cowan some in his mouth and rub the rest on his forehead and chest. If you will walk to the corner there, you will find Mrs. Hislop in a taxi. She will take you to the hospital."

Now the fact was that my wife had been following in a car. However, she had taken great pains to stay out of sight, but her effort was to no avail for, as usual, Baba knew everything. When we reached the hospital with the vibhuthi, Mrs Cowan said, *"Walter took a very bad turn just a little while ago. I thought he was dead, and I was terrified. I at once called Baba in a loud voice. Now, Walter seems a little improved. When I called Baba I felt his presence at once."* At the hospital, Elsie experienced exactly what Baba had told Sri Appa and myself in the car.

Other instances of Baba's powers of resurrection are known to other devotees. The Raja of Ventagiri told me of his experience when, some twenty or so years ago, he witnessed Baba's resurrection of a man dead some six days in whom body decomposition was taking its normal course. About these mysteries, one can make no comment; they are outside the customary human experience.

From Dr. John S. Hislop's book, "My Baba and I", published by Birth Day Publishing Company, San Diego, California.

APPENDIX 3

SAI BABA AND "THE RAINBOW MAN"

This is taken from the charming book by Diana Baskin, "Divine Memories". She and her mother spent many years at Baba's Ashram and her book contains numerous delightful episodes. The incident recorded here concerns her first husband, Joel, and Baba creating a rainbow in response to Joel's doubts when accompanying his wife to Prasanthi Nilayam. It is well known in Sai circles. The rainbow on that day was seen by many people and the unusual configuration was noticed.

Christina was a year and a half old when we left for India. Up to the last minute Joel kept changing his mind and that kept me in a state of suspense until we finally boarded the plane; only then did I feel secure. When we arrived at the ashram, Joel was appalled at the primitive living conditions and grumbled endlessly while we unloaded our luggage. My mother had been in the ashram for a month before we arrived, and as rooms were scarce we shared a room with her. We came well supplied from Bangalore with food, mattresses and everything needed to soften and pamper our spoiled western bodies. I was happy and serene but could see Joel's tension mounting; it needed an outlet. Smoking is not allowed in the ashram so I took him to the hills behind our room, outside the boundaries, to have a smoke.

We sat on a large rock and looked at the view of the valley of Puttaparthi in the late afternoon; it was magnificent. We could see for miles and follow the river below, winding through the peaceful valley surrounded by mountains and deep silence. Suddenly, Joel looked up at the sky and exclaimed, full of wonder and surprise, "Look, look at the rainbow!" I looked up and saw a most peculiar rainbow. It was not curved, but went straight up in the sky and started dissolving slowly from the bottom up while I was looking at it. "What is so interesting about that?" I asked him.

"Don't you remember? That is what I wanted to ask Sai Baba to make for me, a rainbow!" Joel answered a bit shaken I did not reply because I thought Joel's request was absurd. Why should Baba take the trouble to make him a rainbow? Not that I thought He could not make one, but why make such a big thing for such a sceptic? I did not tell Joel my thoughts. I wanted him to believe but strangely enough I did not. Joel looked all around the sky and noticed there were no clouds; it was a perfectly clear day. We had just arrived and not spoken to anyone, so he discarded the possibility that someone could have told Baba that he wanted a rainbow. Only his friends in Los Angeles knew.

When we returned to the room, Professor Kasturi greeted us with the wonderful news that Sai Baba had called us for an interview the following morning. In the morning, we waited in the interview room for Sai Baba to come downstairs. Joel was standing at the foot of the stairs and as Baba reached the bottom, He turned to Joel with a big smile and said, *"Well, character, how did you like my rainbow?"* as He slapped Joel affectionately on the back.

Joel stood speechless, as if frozen, while tears came to his eyes and rolled down his cheeks. Tears and shame overcame me as well when I realised that I was in no position to judge if a person's request was silly, or how deserving anyone is of Baba's grace and love. There is no difference for Baba in making a ring or a rainbow. Nor can any of His manifestations be labelled as "big" or "small," or require "more" or "less" trouble for Him. All of these labels are based on our misconceptions.

Sai Baba sat on a chair and we gathered around Him on the floor; Joel sat at the foot of His chair. Baba turned to a lady from Mexico and said, *"Your knees have been hurting you."* She nodded. Baba glanced at Joel before He carefully pulled up His sleeve as far as it would go

(He often does this for sceptics), and waved His hand in a circular motion. When He turned it upwards there appeared on the palm of His hand, vibhuthi, which He gave to the lady from Mexico.

He then turned to me and asked how my daughter was feeling. I replied, "Not very well." She had a cold and intestinal problems. He again waved His hand and materialised a fresh fig which He told me to give to Christina. The atmosphere was joyous and electric as Baba talked and joked with all of us. During that hour, time stood still and could not be counted. Each moment was eternal. No experience, even the most thrilling I could recall, could compare to the joy of being in His presence. I was beginning to experience a blissful state which grew in intensity as time passed.

When we left the interview room, Joel immediately started his investigation of the fig Baba had materialised. He went to the little village just outside the ashram to see if they were selling figs. He was told that it was not the season for figs; not a single fresh fig could be found anywhere in South India!

Joel told me that when we were in the interview room he was wishing Baba would materialise a fruit the very moment before He did. He had carefully watched Baba's hands during the materialisations and could not detect trickery. Baba had taken him aside for a few moments and privately told Joel things about his life that no one knew and that Joel was not thinking about at the time. Mind reading was out. Joel was becoming fascinated with his "character".

> (Divine Memories of Sathya Sai Baba, Diana Baskin, Birth Day Publishing Company, California, 1990, pp 33-36)

APPENDIX 4

THE ONENESS OF JESUS CHRIST
AND SATHYA SAI BABA

Rev Robert Earl Pipes:

Rev. Robert E. Pipes is an ordained Baptist minister in the U.S. He has played active part in many Government and Church sponsored programmes for the benefit of minority communities in the U.S. He is a consultant to the U.S. Department of Health, Education and Welfare, and is a practicing Pastoral and Psychotherapeutic Counselor. He is also minister to the Temple of God Movement which seeks to help man realize the Divine in him.

Jesus Christ and Sathya Sai Baba are one and the same. Though different manifestations of the same source, the same essence, Jesus Christ is God, the Son, a realized being who earned perfection through self effort of numerous earth lives, and was sent forth from the Father to demonstrate the Divine and to teach mankind how to save itself. And Sathya Sai Baba is God the Father, come from Above. Jesus Christ in his illumination was a manifestation of God in human form. Sathya Sai Baba is God, the Creator, Preserver and Destroyer, the Illuminator of life itself, supremely, universally manifesting in human form, as the Divine Mother and Divine Father.

The activities of Jesus Christ, i.e., his miracles, signs and wonders, his purpose, his mission, his teachings, dawning the first century for the West have since only been paralleled and surpassed in human history by Sathya Sai Baba. Sathya Sai Baba thus fulfils the prophesy of Jesus,

"Truly, truly I say to you, whoever believes in me will do the works that I do and greater works than these he will do because I go to the Father".(John 14 : 12)

Now the Father has come. The impact of Jesus Christ was phenomenal during His one earth-life. The New Testament (Bible) emphasises the three years beginning with his baptism by John the Baptist and culminating with his death, resurrection and ascension. However, other records report an even greater and more extensive work after his resurrection and prior to his discarding his body form. The impact of Sathya Sai Baba is tremendously more phenomenal.

According to the Gospel of St. John,

"Now Jesus did many other signs in the presence of the disciples, which are not written in this book; but these are written that you may believe that Jesus is the Christ, the Son of God, and that believing you may have life in his name". (20: 30, 31) "But there are also many other things which Jesus did; were every one of them to be written, I suppose that the world itself could not contain the books that would be written."(21 : 25)

Thus, the purpose for this Gospel having been written is clear, to convince people of the Divinity of Jesus as the Son of God, and that by believing in him they can experience liberation (salvation). The aim of the book is theological, rather than biographical.

The book, which Biblical scholars believe to have been written around the end of the first century, was orchestrated by Sathya Sai Baba, through a writer who attested authorship to the Apostle John, for the purpose of convincing people, 20 centuries later, of the oneness of Jesus Christ and Sathya Sai Baba, when the Divine Mother-Divine Father would incarnate and expand His work. And, just as John the Baptist was a forerunner proclaiming Jesus as the Christ, so was Jesus Christ, as set forth in the Gospel of St. John, a forerunner, heralding the coming and announcing the life and work of Sathya Sai Baba.

Now devotees of Jesus Christ may follow the teachings of Sathya Sai Baba and realize Jesus Christ or follow the teachings of Jesus Christ and realize Sathya Sai Baba. As Jesus said.

> *"I have been speaking to you in parables - but the time is coming to give up parables and tell you plainly about the Father. When the time comes, you will make your request to Him, in my name, for I need make no promise to plead to the Father for you. for the father himself loves you because you have loved me and have believed that I come from God. Yes, I did come from the Father and I came into the world. Now I leave the world behind and return to the Father."* (John 16 : 25-28)

And earlier in the 14th Chapter, we find these words Philip said to him (Jesus),

> *"Lord, show us the Father, and we shall be satisfied."* Jesus said to him, *"Have I been with you so long, and yet do not know me, Philip ? He who has seen me has seen the Father, how can you say, 'show us the Father?' Do you not believe that I am in the Father and the Father in me? The words that I say to you I do not speak of my own authority; but the Father who dwells in me does his work; or else believe me for the sake of the works themselves."* (Verses 8-11)

Even Jesus's most intimate disciples had difficulty grasping his Divinity and experiencing the oneness of Jesus and the Father. This happened because their faith was overruled at times by their attempt to reason the relationship. Exercises of the mind can only with the greatest, the greatest of difficulty, grasp reality. The path to the heart is the most direct and comprehensible route. Thus, if they could not see the Father in the Son, it is quite understandable that devotees of Jesus Christ may have great difficulty seeing Jesus Christ in the Divine Mother-Divine Father, Sathya Sai Baba.

Why, even John the Baptist, during his imprisonment by Herod, which later followed with his beheading, during an extreme period of frustration, humiliation and aggravation over his plight, sent word to Jesus Christ by one of his (John's) disciples,

> *"are you the one to come or should we look for another?"* (Matthew 11th Chapter)

And Jesus answered him,

> *''Go and tell John what you hear and see: the blind receive their sight and the lame walk, lepers are cleansed and the deaf hear, and the dead are raised up, and the poor have good news preached to them. And blessed is he who takes no offence at me."* (Matthew 11: 4-6)

So if those who were close to Jesus Christ, in their human attempts by human reasoning, failed to see God in Jesus, then today's Christians who use human attempts and human reasoning may not see the Son in the Divine Mother-Divine Father, Sathya Sai Baba.

Said the Christ,

> *"Believe that I am in the Father and the Father in me; or else believe me for the sake of the works themselves."* (John 14 : 11)

Jesus Christ is in Sathya Sai Baba. You can't have one without the other. They are inseparable, The Divine Mother-Divine Father and the Divine Son.

> *"In that day You will know that I am in the Father, and you in me, and I in you."* (John 14 : 20)

[The verb "to believe" is used nearly a hundred times in this Gospel. Faith and knowledge are activities of the human self, in response to Divine revelation, which brings him into the realm of reality. Further, all four Gospels record the saying *"whoever receives me receives him who sent me,"* but in the Gospel of St. John, the phrase *"he who sent me"* is spoken of by Jesus Christ 26 times and a synonymous verb is used 18 times in the Gospel for the Son's mission from the

Father.] from The Interpreter's Bible. from Vol. 8. pg. 438; 442 And Jesus said,

> *"He who hears my words and believes Him who sent me has eternal life; he does not come to judgement but has passed from death to life."* (John 5 : 24.)

Further, Jesus Christ attests to Sathya Sai Baba's profound faith in him:

> *"For I proceeded and came from God; I came not of my own accord, but He sent me. I speak of what I have seen with the Father. He who sent me is true, and I declare to the world what I heard from Him. I do nothing of my own authority but speak thus as the Father taught me. And He who sent me is with me, He has not left me alone, for I always do what is pleasing to him.* (John 8 : 42, 38, 28, 29)

Then there are several other very significant verses which predict the marvel which is upon us today, the advent of Sathya Sai Baba.

> *"Truly, truly, I say to you, he who believes in me will also do the works that I do; and greater works than these he will do, because I go to the Father."*(John 14 : 12)

Jesus taught his disciples how to demonstrate the very power he possessed. Yet, today, and since the early era of Jesus, that knowledge of how to perform the greater works has been lost. And, though a few from time to time have performed a few miracles, none has performed nearly all of the miracles of Jesus Christ nor the *"greater works"* except, Bhagavan (Lord) Sathya Sai Baba. The Divine Mother-Divine Father has come and teaches people how to do the *"works"* of Jesus Christ and the *"greater works"* by doing them Himself. Thus this Scripture is fulfilled. For who believes more in the Son than Sathya Sai Baba, the Divine Mother-Divine Father? For only God in Human Form can teach mankind how to do what Jesus did. For as the Father taught Jesus Christ, so now He has come to teach us all.

Sathya Sai Baba so loved the world that he sent forth a son, Jesus Christ, that whoever believes in him will be saved. And of all who have come to Sathya Sai Baba through Jesus Christ, (See John 3 : 16) Jesus says,

"my sheep hear my voice and I know them, and they know me, and I give them eternal life, and they shall never perish, and no one shall snatch them out of my hand". Then , speaking of Sathya Sai Baba, *"My Father, who has given them to me, is greater than all, and no one is able to snatch them out of the Father's hand. I and the Father are one."* (John 10 : 27-29)

Sathya Sai Baba has come honouring the Son Jesus Christ and also doing the *"greater works"* which Jesus prophesied of those who believe in Him. *"He who has seen the Son has seen the Father."*

May Christians and the whole world recognize this Divine manifestation, the Creator Himself, the Preserver Himself, the Destroyer Himself, has come in the embodiment of Sathya Sai Baba to re-establish the ancient ways, the ancient wisdom, and to destroy evil, that all his children may hurry their return to the Divine essence and bask in the light of TRUTH, PREMA (love), MORALITY AND RIGHTEOUSNESS.

The Lord Sathya Sai Baba is

God the Spirit (John 4 : 24)

The Lord Sathya Sai Baba is

God is Light (I John 1 : 5)

The Lord Sathya Sai Baba is

God is Love (I John 4 : 4)

SPIRIT, LIGHT, LOVE** are the essential being of **Bhagavan Sathya Sai Baba.

> - Abridged from Golden Age 1980, Sri Sathya Sai Books and Publications Trust, Prasanthi Nilayam, India.

THE PILGRIMAGE TO PRASANTHI NILAYAM

Lyn Kriegler is an internationally known illustrator of children's books. In New Zealand she works tirelessly for the promotion of Baba's Values Education in schools. She has visited Baba's Ashram many times, and has willingly agreed to give us this overview of Prasanthi Nilayam as seen through Christian eyes.

Christians making the pilgrimage to Sathya Sai Baba's ashram "Prasanthi Nilayam" in the fast-growing village of Puttaparthi in the Anantapur District of Andhra Pradesh, India, will find a wealth of sights which are evocative of Jesus and His teachings. Foremost would certainly be a visit to the Museum, *Sathya Sai Sanathan Sanskruti* (the Eternal Heritage) inaugurated in November 1990 (see page 118).

This soaring edifice, gracefully situated on a hillside overlooking the ashram, houses three floors of beautiful and inspiring exhibits which embody the history of the great religions and faiths throughout the history of mankind. There are paintings, sculptures, manuscripts, musical instruments, audio-visuals, replicas, scale models, videos, statues, tabloids, recordings and a wide array of miniature chapels and shrines, all expressing the most salient point of Ba ba's teachings: that all religions worship the One and Only God and all reach the same goal.

Places of worship may differ in structure and be known as temples, mosques, churches, etc., but the One who is worshipped therein is the One, the Eternal Spirit, the Supreme Light that forms and nurtures us all, irrespective of caste or creed.

For those who have no particular path or faith, inspiring quotes and photos of great men and women of high intellectual and moral stature are displayed; among them Einstein, Albert Schweitzer, Schopenhauer, Planck and others. A salient feature of the Museum, is the wide range of ways in which human spirituality is expressed.

The first level of the Museum features a breath-taking series of mosaics depicting the life of Christ up -}O the moment of Judas' betrayal. These mosaics duplicate in miniature the mosaic ceiling of the Church of Saint Martin van der Zill in Switzerland. Another feature is a series of clay reliefs showing the Life of Christ.

The second floor features a complete English Chapel, which contains many beautiful statues, icons, a fine Italian Renaissance oil of the Madonna and Child, a large mosaic of St Francis of Assisi, altar treasures from European and Asian churches, plus a collection of Bibles from many time periods and cultures. Of special interest is an unusual silver cross from Italy, which features a Risen Christ against the cross, surrounded by four of the Disciples. Background music selected from the works of Mozart and Bach as well as Gregorian chants lends a hallowed air to the inspiring surroundings.

A monumental figure of Christ stands overlooking the panoramic Vidyagiri Stadium, southeast of the main ashram complex. This statue, standing with arms and palms outstretched (see page 128) is one of six majestic figures now incorporated into the craggy hillside. The other figures are of the Buddha, Lord Krishna, Hanuman, Zoroaster and Lord Shiva. A small temple is alsoincorporated in the hillside alongside these inspiring figures.

A central feature of the ashram complex is the five-sided Lotus Pillar, located in front of the Poornachandra Auditorium (see page 72). This pillar features the emblems of the five major world religions and words from Baba relevant to each. Emblems of the Buddhist, Hindu, Zoroastrian, Muslim and Christian faiths are depicted. The Christian facet displays a Cross and the words *"Cut the 'I' feeling clean across and let your ego die on the cross to endow on you Eternity."* Also known as the *Sarva Dharma Akya Sthoopa,* this commemorative concrete pillar, 50 feet high, was erected on the eve of the Fiftieth Birthday Celebrations of Sathya Sai Baba.

Inside the majestic Poornachandra Auditorium, a series of frescoes depicting scenes from the lives of great figures from the world's religions surround the walls fronting the stage. Jesus as the Good Shepherd features at the left of the centre stage.

At the Sri Sathya Sai Super Specialty Hospital, the entrance foyer, described by one recent visitor as an experience *"comparable to entering the Gates of Heaven themselves',* breathtaking images of Christian devotion are in evidence throughout. Patient wings are designed for people from all faiths; there is a wing depicting motifs from Christ's life, another with scenes from the life of the Buddha, and so on (see page 38).

In addition to these points of interest at the Ashram, it is worth remembering that the vast human wave of visitors flowing at an ever-increasing rate to Puttaparthi brings ministers, priests, monks and nuns, clerics and theologians from all walks of life and all faiths to this inspiring destination.

The village and surrounding landscape of Putt apart hi itself evokes the Holy Land, with its simple huts and whitewashed buildings, the cattle and the donkeys, the arid landscape, and scenes of rural tranquillity. A botanist visiting the area noted that even the wild herbs that grow in the surrounding hillsides are in many instances the same as those which grow around Bethlehem and Jerusalem, and Galilee.

> *"Jesus was Love, Sathya Sai too is Love. That explains the gathering of Christians of all sects which we see here (at Prasanthi Nilayam). In Rome today Catholics gather to celebrate the birth of Jesus. The Protestants celebrate it by themselves in their churches. The Jews are not welcomed anywhere, but in the presence of Sathya Sai, all are equally welcome. The Jews*

arraigned Jesus, and demanded that He should be punished. In this (Sai) Presence, Jews are adoring that very Jesus. The Love of Sathya Sai has transformed and transcended those memories.

Sathya Sai Baba

CHRISTMAS AT PRASANTHI NILAYAM

Christians from all parts of the world and all walks of life arrive at Prasanthi Nilayam during the days leading up to Christmas to experience a celebration of the Birth of Christ quite unlike any other in the world. Baba has said that the day one truly celebrates Christmas is the day when the Spirit of Christ is born in your own heart. He says that it should be a day spent in prayer, holy thoughts and sacred activity rather than drinking, feasting and giving of gifts.

Christmas in Puttaparthi has been, for millions, their first experience of the true meaning of Christmas. Preparations begin around the 10th of December. With the first groups of visitors arriving, plans begin for the presentation of the yearly children's Christmas play, featuring the Nativity and a theme which explores the meaning of Christmas. A large choir begins to assemble, with musicians and orchestral co-ordinators from all over the world. Anyone can take part in these activities.

At this time, a large hall is decorated for all the overseas visitors to use as a Satsang (Fellowship) Hall. This hall is used daily for musical and choral presentations from an array of international cultures. Events occur which profoundly move many hearts, such as a recent presentation by Jewish and German visitors, and a rousing, joyous round of Zulu singing by an African group. These events take place daily in the weeks leading up to Christmas Day.

On Christmas Eve a fully orchestrated international choir presents a concert of Christmas carols in Baba's presence, and more of the same on Christmas Day. Early on Christmas Morning, visitors assemble outside the Mandir (main temple) at 5 am to form a candlelight procession moving through the ashram grounds singing *"Silent Night "*, *"Away in a Manger"* and other timeless Christmas carols.

Hindus, Buddhists and Moslems are seen joining in for what is always a heart-warming gathering around the Mandir balcony, for Baba appears from the twin silver doors at the conclusion of the starlit procession with His hands raised in blessing as the singers break into *"Joy to the World"*.

Later in the day visitors gather in the Poornachandra Auditorium to hear noted speakers and Baba Himself discourse on the true meaning of this sacred day. Over the years, Baba has given many fresh insights into the life of Christ and His teachings in these Christmas Discourses. After Baba's discourse the Children's Christmas Play is presented, to an assembly which can number into the tens of thousands. Children from all over the world are involved in this always-delightful half-hour event, with sets, costumes, lighting, special effects and music, all provided by the overseas visitors.

The play culminates with Baba Himself coming up to share the stage with a very, very happy crowd of' beaming children for the encore (see page 152). At the end of the event, the overseas visitors are treated to a delicious vegetarian Christmas dinner-complete with ice cream!

Lyn Kriegler

"At Prasanthi Nilayam every day is a Festival Day; every day is a Holy Day. As the saying goes, it is 'Perpetual Joy, Perpetual Green.' This Day (Christmas) is associated with the birth and life of Jesus. It is a good occasion to give up the old and welcome the new thought, word and deed Jesus was the Embodiment of compassion and love. His heart melted in sympathy when He saw anyone suffering. His entire life was dedicated to service. In the interests of Truth, He laid down His own life. Such persons are revered in the world, however much times change."

Sathya Sai Baba

APPENDIX 6

PRISON BREAK

This section includes the text from a web page:

http://media.radiosai.org/journals/Vol_06/01MAR08/04-
newzealand.htm

The original web page may be found by entering into a search engine *"Sai Baba Peter Phipps prison break."* It would be worthwhile to view the original source. While the words of the two prisoners are faithfully copied, there have been embellishments of my original copy.

PRISON BREAK!

Sai's Love Breaks Barriers at a Prison in New Zealand

Even as humanity remains embroiled in its daily struggles of survival and success, the most mysterious, sacred and potent presence on the face of the planet in the Divine Self of Sri Sathya Sai Baba continues to awaken the God in millions of hearts, in thousand different ways, in places close and very far from the seat of His Physical Presence – Prasanthi Nilayam, India. The first ever Divine Incarnation of international influence during His very lifetime, the story of the Sai Avatar continues to elude human comprehension. Yet, never for a moment does He stop in the holy task He has come to foster - to remind each of us of our own divine nature; that everyone is God and all is one.

Baba says: **"My Reality is unreachable. Unreachable it will be not only today but even for a thousand years, even if a thousand years are spent in ardent enquiry by all the people of the world in active unison. But the Bliss emanating from My Reality is within the reach of all the nations of the Universe and you can partake of it. My mystery, My Power can never be understood."**

True to His words, this chronicle is yet another little episode from the love revolution initiated by a little village boy on 20th Oct 1940in a remote place called Uravakonda, in rural India that has turned into a tidal wave, a global love tsunami, sweeping millions of seekers off their feet from corporate America to prisons in New Zealand!

The current feature is a story of the most unexpected of spiritual seekers who are experiencing the bliss of Bhagavan Baba's Reality in the least likely of locations, proving that God realization is not limited to such places as churches, temples, mosques, synagogues or the caves of the Himalayas.

Bill and Arthur are two prison inmates whose cells are their seats of sacred and intense spiritual discipline. The Cosmic Consciousness that is personified in the person of Sri Sathya Sai Baba has revealed itself to them right there, inside the prison. Mr. Peter Phipps is a prison counsellor who became the chosen instrument of God in taking the Avatar's message to these two inmates.

This account, possibly startling to some, only due to the limitations of human rationality, comes to you from all three men involved. It is woven in three distinct voices to bring you each of their individual experiences, proving that the tales of God's Glory elucidated in the Bhagavatham, the Bible and the Quran are daily occurrences in the career of the current Avatar. For every single recorded instance of His mind-boggling Powers, there are a million others that no one knows of, for such is the Glory of the Lord of the Universe, fondly referred to as Swami by His devotees.

In a landmark discourse on October 24, 1993, Swami said:

"Very soon the Glory of Sai will spread to every part of the world. It will increase a thousand fold. The reason is the essential goodness of the Sai Mission. It is totally free from any taint.

Every act is done out of the purest of motives. Everything that is said is based on Truth. All activities are conducted without depending on any outsider. Hence, there is no room for fear.

After the harvest, when the sheaves of grains are winnowed, the wind blows away all the chaff, leaving only the grains behind. Through this process, the true devotees will remain steadfast. The wavering puppets will drift away. This is the process of winnowing."

My name is Peter Phipps and this is the story of my path to prison ministry in New Zealand. I studied psychology while at University and gained a postgraduate degree in this subject. For practical experience, I joined the Probation Service in 1961 and was later invited to become a prison psychologist in 1962. I enjoyed the former job but hated the latter. The Prison Service had grand formal objectives of rehabilitation, reformation and transformation of prisoners. In practice, it was a hotbed of negativity, destruction, anger and malevolence. I left it around 1968; I was a broken and disillusioned man.

In the intervening years I observed prison policy and practice in New Zealand with some level of cynicism and despair. I knew that the high-sounding statements of politicians, publicly stated, were far from the truth.

I first heard of Swami from an American hippie around 1975, but coming from a man who had once been into LSD and other mind-altering drugs, I was sceptical of his claim of having met God in flesh and blood. However, he introduced me to a form of meditation on light that I found very positive and especially helpful at a later time, as we shall see. The meditation is similar to what Ms. Phyllis Krystal teaches.

I was active within the Christian church, on and off, over the years, and obtained work with the Salvation Army in 1989. In 1990, I attended a course for Victim Support offered by two Americans. Included in the course was a half-day workshop on mass murder counselling. The course members protested that these things do not happen in New Zealand, but the trainers insisted that this was part of their training.

Ten days later, we had a mass killing at Aramoana, a small settlement near Dunedin in the South Island. I received a call asking whether I would be prepared to drop everything and join a team of three to work with survivors and the community. I was quite apprehensive about the job, but due to Swami's Grace, we had been recently trained for just such an event. I am sure this was no coincidence. On the flight down, I started the light meditation, which I often used as a form of spiritual protection and support, and I asked God for His help, as I knew I could not do the job in my own strength.

Immediately, I felt a powerful presence of Love and Wisdom and felt a strong current of energy flowing around us. This energy stayed with us all for the whole time we were working. Everyone on the team felt the energy and had the same experience. In the short time on the ground, we saw many miracles of healing happening before us.

While giving thanks to God after the event, I heard an internal voice say, *"I am greater than you know, seek Me out and find Me."* I started to enquire if there was anything about Jesus that I did not know. I started in a book shop dealing with "New Age" type of books, and in a few minutes, one book almost leapt off the shelf into my hand. It was "The Jesus Mystery" by Janet and Richard Bock. The book looks first at the life of Jesus and then describes Swami. I knew I had found what I was looking for. However, given my scientific bent of mind, I first tried to prove Swami could not be who He says He is, but I was unable to find any fault in Him. Subsequently, I made several trips to Prasanthi Nilayam.

Reconciling Christian Beliefs with Sai Spirituality

In an interview with Swami, I put the question to Him: *"How do we present Your message to Christians?"* He replied: *"Do not teach Sai Baba, teach Jesus Christ. But teach that Jesus taught Universal Love."* He added a beautiful mini discourse on the nature of Love, concluding *"only Love for God is Bhakti or devotion."*

I became a lay minister in my Church and accepted other positions of leadership, and taught about Jesus in the way Swami had directed me. I undertook a diploma level course in theology and Christian history. I became well-known beyond the boundaries of my parish because of my work in opposing the building of casinos and gambling facilities.

I was the Director of a weekend Cursillo (short course in Christian living) and got talking to Audrey Moonlight, the wife of one member of my team, who was involved in prison ministry. She told me that a "Faith Based Unit" was being established at a nearby prison and that they were looking for mentors and group leaders. After my earlier experience with prisons, I hoped that this would be an exciting idea that should prove to be a more positive experience this time around. So I applied for both opportunities and was appointed as one of four group facilitators in 2003, and joined the team working under a contract with Prison Fellowship New Zealand.

Many Voices, One Song; Many Faiths, One God

While the leaders and other facilitators of the team are Christians of a rather fundamentalist group who believe that "the only way to God is through Jesus Christ", I am quietly more universal in my teaching.

At different times we have had Moslems and Buddhists in the groups. We are supposed to convert them into Christians, but I liked to point out to the Buddhists how the teachings of Jesus and Buddha are the same, and start a session with "Allah-O-Akbar" when Moslems were present.

It is always my objective to help them take one step towards God in whatever form they expect Him to be, just as Bhagavan Baba has taught us that paths are many, but goal is one.

Our sessions are intended to be based on the Bible, and some prisoners expect me to produce a Biblical reference for every statement I make.

Other prisoners ask questions beyond the general framework of the Bible, and I am happy to talk to them on any question, provided it is spiritual.

Divine Energy Pervades Prison

At Aramoana, I experienced Swami as a great current of Energy flowing through me to others. There are times in the prison that the same experience occurs. The Energy sometimes seems so strong that I feel I am plugged into the electricity mains. I notice this is always a time when someone has a need for something as basic as forgiveness for their crimes or support in times of grief. It is beyond my control, but happens when I open myself to Swami in my efforts to help the man.

There have been times when the presence of God seems extraordinarily strong and profound. At these times there is often a period of conflict and difficulty as too many men take the spiritual energy to their ego and regard themselves as "the best Christian in the unit". Then there may be fights as to who it is that speaks for God. Ego is the great enemy in the prison, as much as in any place else.

At present we are going through a time when there is very strong spiritual energy in the unit, with many of the men undergoing transforming experiences or great blessings. I urge the men to keep quiet about what has happened so as not to give rise to jealousy in the other men. Many of the events we might recognise as miracles go unnoticed as a result.

I do not speak openly about Swami, but always present His message in combination with a Biblical text, which it is easy to do.

Gayatri Mantra, the Universal Prayer

Some men ask me, in private, questions of spiritual nature that go beyond Christian orthodoxy.

They may be along the lines of past lives and *karma*. In response, I give them material from various sources, possibly including Swami, without mentioning the name. When the questions are persistent and sincere, I may give them a book about Swami or a printed discourse that answers the question. This is when the moment of Truth arises!

There is an inmate, a man whom we shall call Arthur. He asked me some very searching questions that I could only answer with reference to Swami. I started giving him some material and he kept asking for more. He told me that he was having trouble meditating so I gave him a book from the UK on light meditation. I followed it up with information on the Gayathri Mantra and a CD with Swami chanting the Gayathri Mantra 108 times. He started to chant the Gayathri Mantra with Swami each morning, and very soon Swami began to visit him in his cell several times. On his own volition he became a vegetarian and had a battle with the prison administration to change his diet.

Explaining the sudden inner transformation he underwent due to his Divine tryst with Bhagavan Baba, Arthur says: *"I was first introduced to Sathya Sai Baba by a devotee, Peter Phipps, who was facilitating the Christian group programme in the Faith Based Unit in a New Zealand prison, where I am at the moment serving time for drug offences.*

By the time I met Peter I was determined to find the meaning and reason for my existence. I asked him for information on some of the spiritual questions I had. He presented me with materials either by Swami or about Swami to read.

When I began to study the materials and the teachings of Swami, I was so struck by the Universal Truth they teach. This really motivated me into more inquiry about Swami. I was very blessed because Peter was always gracious to answer my questions. I spent a long time with him in talks about his experience with Swami. This was the beginning of everything for me.

As a prisoner, I have a lot of time to study, meditate, and practice the teachings of Swami. I prayed to Him to help me transform my life and to cultivate love for Him. He answered my prayers and changed my life in a very profound way. I am deeply grateful for His love. Looking back, I realised that He has always been there and has always protected me."

Since I used to sometimes bring Sai literature to answer Arthur's queries, one day as I was photocopying some pages from Sanathana Sarathi for him, I spoiled the first page by inserting it the wrong way into my copier. It had a picture of Swami, in colour, together with an extract from the discourse. I would never destroy a sacred image of Swami and wondered what to do with it. I was prompted to take it in to Arthur. When I went into the prison that day, Arthur told me "*Swami told me to ask for a picture of Him*". I told Arthur I had the picture with me. He was overwhelmed. Since then he has made a frame for the picture and the quote and displays it in his cell. Several other prisoners as well as custodial staff note the picture and the Divine quotation and ask Arthur about it. Several staff members as well as his fellow prisoners are drawn to the picture and ponder on the wisdom of the words.

Experiencing the Father and the Holy Son on Christmas

Before last Christmas, Arthur was on a three-day fast and was hungry. He was also concerned about finding sufficient money to buy noodles as a present for all the 60 prisoners in his unit, but did not have enough funds. He had managed to have only 54 packets of noodles and was trying to decide who should not get a packet. On the second day of his fast, on December 23, as he was praying, his cell filled with a bright light and he opened his eyes to see Swami dressed in white, holding up bleeding palms.

Swami told Arthur that he and Jesus Christ are the same. He said Jesus had transcended body consciousness and did not feel pain during the Crucifixion. He told Arthur to complete the fast and that he would no longer feel hunger.

Addressing his other concern, Swami also told Arthur to distribute the noodles to all and assured him that there would be sufficient to go around. When Arthur enlisted the help of a friend, another inmate, whom we shall refer to as Bill, to distribute the noodles, he pointed out that they were insufficient for everyone. Yet when Arthur and Bill got together again, they were astonished to find that every man in the unit received a packet and there were eleven left over!

I requested both the prison inmates concerned - Arthur and Bill, to share their individual reflections of the experience.

Arthur says: *One early morning of November last year [2007] I was chanting Gayatri in my prison cell. I still had about 30 to go when the prison staff came around to unlock the cells. I prayed to Swami to please help me to finish before the staff gets here. The time was 7.15 am. I finished the mantras before the door was unlocked and the time was still 7.15 am. I couldn't believe what was happening. I felt like time was standing still.*

This experience, coupled with the previous occasions when Swami has appeared to me, left me with a deep sense of love and devotion to Him. As I continue with my sadhana, Swami has come several times into my cell and talked to me. Ever since I became aware of His Divine Presence in my life, it has been like coming home to where I belong.

Before Christmas I decided to undertake a three day fast to help me to clear some issues I had with the person of Jesus Christ and Swami. I gave my food to the others with joy because I knew that Swami would take care of me.

On the second day of my fast, December 23 [2007], I was feeling very hungry physically and was in hunger pain too.

I was on my knees praying to Swami in my cell when suddenly I felt a powerful presence with me.

I stopped praying and opened my eyes and to my astonishment the room was lit with brilliant white and blue light and the cell seemed to dissolve as there was nothing existing except myself and Swami dressed in white and smiling beautifully. At this moment I had lost the sense of myself. He held up His hands, from which blood was coming from the palms. He was speaking to me but He was not making any sound and yet I could understand what He was saying.

He said that He and Christ are the same. He told me that Christ did not suffer on the Cross, as there was no body consciousness. He told me also to continue and finish the fasting and that from that point I would not feel any more hunger pains [this proved to be true].

As this was going on, there was no sense of time or body. I could not tell how long this experience lasted. When He left, I returned to the body and my cell and I was not feeling anything but total transformation and joy. This was the most wonderful experience I have ever had in my life.

I had decided before Christmas 2007 that I would present my brothers in the Unit with me with a packet of noodles as a Christmas present. I had been purchasing noodles out of my prison wages. I was quite concerned that despite sacrificial saving from my meagre prison earnings there was not sufficient money to buy for all the men in the Unit.

I decided that I and my closest friends would have to go without. On the morning of the Christmas day, I called my friend Bill, and asked him to help with distributing the noodles to the men. We prayed to Swami and told Him to bless the gift and that we are just an instrument to be used to distribute it. I handed a bundle of packets to Bill and told him to distribute them to a group of prisoners, but that there would be none for him as they were not sufficient.

I distributed the rest of the food. Bill and I came back in astonishment. We had distributed the food to all those designated and not only was there enough for all, but there were about 11 packets left over.

We could not explain it. I recognised at once that Swami had multiplied the food. I was overjoyed at this example of Swami's Love, Omnipresence and Omnipotence.

Bill, who distributed the food with me, was aware that Swami had multiplied the food and was transformed by this experience and has become a devotee as well.

I have also noticed that several men who ate the Divinely multiplied food have made dramatic transformations in their characters."

Bill, the other inmate at the same facility, has also become a devotee of Swami. He also chants the Gayathri Mantra108 times each morning. Another man since then has told me that Christ has appeared in his cell and asked for material about Swami. Bill explains what he makes of the Divine phenomenon occurring in the prison in New Zealand.

Bill says*: "I grew up thinking that miracles are the stuff of the Bible, never to be manifest in our time. I have come to know of the Being we call Sai Baba, and the miracles He performs for His devotees. The first time I heard of Swami I knew that He was who He said He is. But like most, I had to pass through the mental barrier I had placed upon myself, believing that only Christ can perform such miracles. Swami has helped me to see that He and Christ are the same Being, manifest in different physical bodies, and that with God there is no limit. The more I read about Swami, His teachings and the miracles performed, I began to truly believe that God cannot be restricted to what we conceive "Him" to be.*

"We believe that nothing is impossible for God, but we are always reluctant to believe that He can do all that He says He is capable [of]. We pray for miracles each day but when a "man" in India begins to perform the very same miracles, we are quick to dismiss them as a trick or an illusion. The illusion is our ignorance of who God truly is. My journey with Christ has shown me that miracles are a natural state of an enlightened man - He that has attained Christ Consciousness, Buddha-hood or closeness with God. When in this stage, miracles are a natural state for the created [man], then isn't it child's play for God Incarnate?

Going back to Bill's account of the experience where the food multiplied, he recorded the following in his reflection:

"I am currently a prisoner at a Christian Faith Unit, and last Christmas I was witness to a miracle performed by Swami. Brother Arthur had

purchased noodle packets from our canteen to distribute as a gesture of goodwill to the brothers at this festive time. The noodles purchased were not enough for all.

At this time, Brother Arthur was fasting for three days prior to Christmas [2007] and Swami appeared to him during meditation. Swami's instructions were to distribute the noodles [to all the inmates of the unit] and there will be enough [for all]. Brother Arthur asked me to help distribute the noodles on Christmas Day, and sure enough, there was enough for all and some left over. The two of us discussed this chain of events and truth be told. Neither of us was surprised, reason being, when one is surrendered to the Will of God, and works with undying love in their heart for the Lord and fellow brothers, such 'unnatural' acts occur. I realise that this miracle happened because of Swami's Grace, and in my heart I thanked Swami for the blessing and my love for Him grew even stronger.

For me, Swami was manifesting these miracles for the persona of Jesus, the Christ, 2000 years ago, and He is manifesting the same miracles at this time in the persona of Sri Sathya Sai Baba."

Today, my work as a prison counsellor is still evolving, and lately at a more rapid pace. Five men so far have been told of Swami and all accept Him for who He claims to be, but not all yet feel called to practice His teachings. Only two of the five could be described as committed devotees. They need nurturing, and Swami is ensuring that they get what is needed, whether by appearing in person or telling them to "ask Peter".

I need to be careful because due to their limited understanding of Swami's Universal Message, which is all inclusive and validates every one of Jesus' teachings, my fellow facilitators may mistakenly conclude that I am fostering a non-Christian religion or philosophy.

It is interesting that many custodial staff and prisoners are open to Universal Truth as being more sensible as the narrower "Jesus is the only way to God" line that we are supposed to teach.

I have no doubt that Swami is richly blessing this work and is preparing some men to be great ambassadors for Him both in prison and after release.

Intense Yearning - Key to Spiritual Success

Interestingly, a large part of the success of the project is that prisoners generally have a great spiritual hunger. Many suffer from acute feelings of guilt and remorse. Many genuinely want to change themselves to avoid coming back to prison or to become better fathers or husbands. I have found that in parish work in the community, there is not the same level of hunger or dissatisfaction with themselves as to who or what they are. People only ask for feeding when they are hungry, and one does not find this level of spiritual hunger in the community.

The multiplication of Swami's grace through the unit is, truly, leaving me quite stunned. Those lads with their intense *sadhana*, application of Swami's teachings and their hunger for Truth would leave most of us ashamed. They are getting the Grace they deserve.

Apart from the few we have been discussing, the rest of the unit is extraordinarily gracious. When, a few months ago, the prison system had to increase the lockdown hours due to staff shortages, the men rejoiced and held a service of thanksgiving. Other units experienced various degrees of anger. The men are now locked down for 15 hours per day in single cells.

There are over 20 units in the prison complex, but I am hearing that the level of violence is now decreasing in the other units.

I have had the sense for a long time that we can start a spiritual revolution in Unit 7 that would then be taken out to the subculture which largely forms our criminal population. Once the revolution starts with those at the bottom of the social pyramid, it should then extend to the rest of the country. I think we are seeing the start of it. Swami once told a New Zealand group that in time to come "New Sailand" will provide and example of stability to an unstable world.

Grateful to be His Instrument of Change

To be an instrument for Swami's Mission is a great privilege and I recommend Sai devotees should consider whether they, also, should be ministering to those in prison. What better way to explain the joy of my bonding with fellow aspirants, my brothers in the prison, than by quoting what Arthur has to say of Swami's presence in his life?

Arthur says: "

I shall conclude with a short passage from the Bible:

"Then the King will say to those on his right, 'Come, you who are blessed by my Father; take your inheritance, the Kingdom prepared for you since the creation of the world. For I was hungry and you gave Me something to eat, I was thirsty and you gave Me something to drink, I was a stranger and you invited Me in, I needed clothes and you clothed Me, I was sick and you looked after Me, I was in prison and you came to visit Me.'

"Then the righteous will answer Him, 'Lord, when did we see You hungry and feed You, or thirsty and give You something to drink? When did we see You a stranger and invite You in or needing clothes and clothe You? When did we see You as sick or in prison, and go to visit You?'

"The King will reply, 'I tell you the Truth, whatever you did for one of the least of these brothers of Mine, you did for Me.' (Matthew 25:34-40)

☐ Names have been changed for prisoner privacy

EPILOGUE

On my third visit to Prasanthi Nilayam in January/February 1994, I was fortunate to be part of a group led by a great devotee, Mata Betty. Our group had two interviews with "Swami". I offered to Sathya Sai Baba a close-to-final draft of this book to sign. As He took the pen and put it to the paper, there was a lifting of all the doubts I had ever had about whether this book is the Lord's Will. I felt also validated in the work I have been doing in His Name.

In the first interview, Sathya Sai Baba manifested Vibhuthi, golden earrings and a gold ring for various members of the group. I have personally never had any doubts that these manifestations are not produced by conjuring, but other people I have spoken to are not prepared to accept such statements on trust. I had seen His manifestations in the past, but from a distance. I can now testify, personally, that these items are produced by Him out of thin air.

Sathya Sai Baba made it plain in the interview that He knew all the details of our lives, including those we might have preferred to keep secret. At times he chuckled like a small child when a person appeared astonished when their thoughts were being conveyed to the group. He made it clear in these small ways that He is Omniscient, Omnipresent and Omnipotent. He also displayed enormous Love and Compassion, being very gentle and sometimes even tender.

On the second interview, I asked Him "Swami, how should one go about presenting your message to Christians?" Sathya Sai Baba replied *"Do not teach Sai Baba, teach Jesus Christ. But tell them that Jesus Christ taught Universal Love, Love for all without distinction. Jesus said, 'All are One, be alike to everyone '. There are many groups of Christians, each saying that their God is the only true God They make God so small."* At this point, Swami clenched His right fist and held it out. He continued, *"God is not small, He is Universal Love."* Swami elaborated, *"There are many kinds of love. Love for a child is mixed with possessiveness, love for a wife is mixed with lust. Only love for God is Bhakthi (pure devotion without egoism)* ".

My experience is that when Sathya Sai Baba talked to me, there was total attention on me, which in itself is a fantastic experience. I have never experienced such attention before.

As the second interview ended, and Swami made towards the door, I opened the door for Him, and He gave me a playful pat on the cheek. At that touch, I went into bliss. I value that touch more than any degrees, honours or possessions. For me, that light touch is the only miracle I need from Sathya Sai Baba.

OM SAI RAM
Peter Phipps

ADDENDUM

After the first edition of the current book was published I found myself in a dispute with some American Anglicans who tried to convince me that what I was writing could not be true. At the time I knew that what Jesus and Sai Baba taught were the same, but this conflicted with the official teaching of the Church. I was puzzled by this.

These Christians suggested I look at the Church Councils of Nicaea, Constantinople, and Trent to see what the Church was teaching. Having attended several Synods, and observing how debates are structured within the Church I had a good idea of the politics involved. I also studied Church history and took a course in Education for Ministry. I then felt I understood the issues involved and wrote a second book *"Greater Than You Know"*, covering much the same material as in this book, but from a theological and critical perspective.

In 1996 I took a group to Whitefield, near Bangalore to Swami's ashram at Brindavan. Included in the group were an Anglican priest and his wife. Swami called us an interview and manifested a ring for the priest, bearing the image of Shirdi Sai Baba. I took the draft of my second book and He indicated He would bless it later, which happened in 1998.

My last pilgrimage to Prashanti Nilayam was in 2008. As always it was an amazing experience.

FOR FURTHER READING

I suggest that anyone wanting to know more about Sathya Sai Baba, would find much valuable information in the following books. Hundreds of books about Him are available in almost every language and more are constantly being produced, but the following are some of the best known and probably the most comprehensive. Your local Sai Centre would know where you can conveniently obtain them.

Baskin, Diana, *"Divine Memories of Sathya Sai Baba "*, Birth Day Publishing Company, California, 1990

Bock, Janet, *"The Jesus Mystery of Lost Years and Unknown Travels "*. Aura Books, Los Angeles, 1980

Hislop, Dr John S, *"My Baba and I "*, Sri Sathya Sai Books and Publications Trust, Prasanthi Nilayam, India, and Birth Day Publishing Co., San Diego, California.

Hislop, Dr John S, *"Conversations with Bhagavan Sri Sathya Sai Baba "*, Sri Sathya Sai Books and Publications Trust, Prasanthi Nilayam, India, and Birth Day Publishing Co., San Diego, California.

Kasturi, N, *"Loving God"*, Sri Sathya Sai Books and Publications Trust, Prasanthi Nilayam, India

Krystal, Phyllis, *"Sai Baba the Ultimate Experience "*, Sawbridge Enterprises Limited, London, 1985

Murphet, Howard, *"Sai Baba Man of Miracles "*, Vrindavanum Books, London, 1971

Murphet, Howard, *"Walking the Path with Sai Baba"* Samuel Weiswer, Inc., York Beach, Maine, U.S.A.

Murphet Howard, *"Sai Baba Avatar"* Birth Day Publishing Co., San Diego, California